Horus Templar

and the

Case of the Wimpy War-Criminal

E.L. WARD

Horus Templar and the Case of the Wimpy War-Criminal is a work of fiction. Names, characters, places, and incidents either are the product of the author's imagination or are used fictitiously. Any resemblance to actual persons, living or dead, events, or locales is entirely coincidental.

ISBN: 978-1-7370436-0-7

Table of Contents

"To be proud is to nurture a conceit – to assert a delusion. And those who are delusional go to great lengths to protect their delusions. They will often strive against reason. When pressed, they may even be made to strive against themselves."

- Magormissahr, *Referendums on the World, Vol. 332*

Chapter 1

Dark and stormy was the night.

Deputy Constable Stenya Miloje unfurled his umbrella into the deluge, reaching with his other hand for the extended arm of one of his sergeants. With the help of the sturdy youngster, he hauled his aching old bones out of the dry carriage, good shoes splashing down onto the cobblestone, his feet instantly soaked. He grumbled something unintelligible from beneath the large mustache his office obliged him to maintain, even as he adjusted his equally obligatory bobby. The weather and the hour were staunchly set against him.

But once he straightened up – even in soggy socks – the protest of his body washed away, old eyes flashing with the intensity of the lightning in the air as he accepted an umbrella from his sergeant. This wasn't a call he had to make. But when word reached him of what was being brought in from the far side of Mt. Norvein, he decided it was well worth dragging himself out of bed in the middle of the night, just to be present. A grizzled veteran on the force, the conceit that he had 'seen it all' was natural. Tonight, however, that sentiment was not to be found. Tonight, he would see something *new*. Something few, if any, who lived in Jast-Madiir had ever seen, and lived to tell about...

It was coming now, from up the road. The streetlamps had been doused in the heavy downpour, so that he could hardly make out the approaching caravan. But he could certainly *hear* it... a dozen, perhaps two-dozen horses marching in step. The thing they were bringing had a cavalry section escort by now, he was told. Never mind it had been captured by just one man and his wife in the first place. On top of that, it was supposed to be injured in some way. Even so, Miloje understood the importance of making a minor military spectacle of all this, of course. It was the closest the cavalry, infantry, or any other division had ever come to claiming a victory over their firmly-entrenched, savage neighbors...

Well before the prisoner's party pulled into view, a tall gangly fellow emerged into the pool of light under the entryway to St. Argonsburg Civil HQ, approaching Miloje with his long, purposeful stride. He closed the distance before Miloje even had a chance for more private grumbling, tipping his new bobby. "Constable," he greeted Miloje with a smile. It was Captain Alexei – recently promoted and transferred from Podunkville –

some little rural nowhere that Miloje had never heard of before, until Alexei had been brought around to prattle about it incessantly...

"That's *Deputy* Constable to you, boy," Miloje admonished the youngster, eyeing him with uncertainty. The Captain didn't have an umbrella with him, though he was certainly important enough to carry one. In the cold damp, an officer ought to be better outfitted. But always, the lad seemed to be trying to prove himself somehow. Perhaps, in the week to come, he hoped to demonstrate how well he could do his job while dealing with walking pneumonia...

"Right you are sir, and may I not soon forget it," Alexei said, undeterred. Having greeted his superior, he promptly spun on his heel. This was something he clearly did not mean to miss, either. "Rather remarkable, this occasion, isn't it?" he asked over his shoulder. "I can assure you, we never have anything like this happen back in little old Podunkville."

Miloje rolled his eyes. "Not in St. Argonsburg, either, Captain. We're all witnessing a bit of history here."

As the Deputy Constable continued to scan the whole scene, if only by habit, he chanced to notice a dim light flickering in a high window of the Civil complex. Even in the dead of night, he knew the window well enough. It was the viewport of the District Attorney's personal office. And standing in it, gazing down, was a sharp, canine silhouette, blacker than midnight...

"That we are, sir," Captain Alexei agreed at length. "Looks like even Mr. Blackforest thinks so."

"Ah, you noticed him, too," Miloje retorted, actually a bit impressed. "Perhaps there's hope for you yet, son."

A bolt rent the air, revealing the iron-barred carriage and its escort in a momentary flashbulb, already closer than his ears had made it. Thunder pealed, and Miloje heard the horses of his own carriage quietly whinny their displeasure. As the caravan pulled up alongside the Civil Headquarters building, a gang of newsmen slunk out of the shadows and crowded in around the steps, pens out and eager to jot down the short, spartan sentences that would comprise tomorrow's papers...

This was the big moment.

He watched as three of the stoutest cavalrymen dismounted and approached the carriage where the hostage was penned-up. They unlocked the heavy door, and the lead man drew a shortsword, cautiously entering the utter blackness of the mobile cell. After a few breathless moments of watching, Miloje saw *something else* emerge. A large gunny sack was rolled to the doorway, seeming to wriggle under its own power. The two men still on the ground spent a couple awkward beats trying to decide where to grab, then began hoisting the living luggage out into the rain, with the third man supporting the parcel as he followed behind it.

Miloje winced. Even with a bit of dread-imagination, he couldn't make the sack – or the creature within – out to be all that big. Going by size alone, he supposed one man alone could probably have hefted it...

The one thing that really seemed to justify all that manpower was the *squirming*. By now, the bag was really trying to fight back. It flopped, it contorted, it batted, and, at intervals, fairly exploded. And all the while, there was other-worldly clicking and screeching. Here, the Deputy Constable found some payoff for the curiosity that had brought him forth in this uncreatorly hour. Nothing Human – nor even remotely shaped like a Human – could thrash in a gunny sack the way this feral thing was doing...

But before he half knew it, the military men had their hostage up the stairs, through the army of journalists, and into the Headquarters. Miloje found himself absently staring in the rain, lips pursed, with naught left to do but reflect on the incredibly brief episode...

"What a shame," Captain Alexei said, rubbing some fog out of his spectacles with his sleeve. "We didn't get to *see* it. Not really, anyway."

The Deputy Constable nodded, still looking straight on. The Captain seemed to know well enough that this case was going to be above even his now-impressive pay grade. Miloje himself would handle the police side of things: The interrogation, and the gathering of all prudent evidence... if any was in fact called for. He reached up to give the Captain a consolatory pat on the shoulder. "If a gracious mood should come upon me unwanted, I may let you see it yet, my lad. But I'm not sure they'll believe you, when you write home to Podunkville about this." He snorted to himself. "Who would have ever thought that any of us should bear witness to one of the phantom tribesmen, brought to answer for his peoples' hostilities at last?"

He shook his head in final disbelief.

"A Dire Mantid."

Chapter 2

His clawed hand reached out to steady the stemmed glass in front of him just in time as the moaning of the brakes and the lonesome howl of the whistle split the night air. Hard light poured through the blinders of his car windows, crossing the room in frantic streaks. They slowed, until at last he was looking down at a slatted pool of light before his door, watching as the water gushing down outside made endless waves of distortion. Melancholy, muted trumpet music from three cars ahead swirled like a haze in the shadows where he sat...

The sullen Public Defender plucked the glass from his desk and took another sip of the grape juice – incidentally, the *last* sip. Settling back into his office chair, he grunted a dissatisfied grunt to himself. Having completed the train's long circuit, he knew dawn was near, even if the dense rainclouds prolonged the deepest dark. He'd passed another restless night, haunted by the knowledge that there was all kinds of justice to do out there... and he wasn't doing any of it...

He ran a hand down his face and long snout. He could feel his eyelids and jowls drooping under their own weight. But sleeping now was irrelevant. Perhaps as irrelevant as being awake.

He goaded himself to stand up and shake the stagnancy out of his massive, robust frame. And then, not conscious of any reason, he walked over to the window facing the boarding side of the train, holding a pair of blinds apart with the ends of his claws, peering out with a tired but vigilant eye.

His other eye opened in sudden surprise.

Standing below, astride his car, was a young Mesomela woman. She was staring straight back up at him as Humans bustled by on all sides. Her dark visage was blotted out under the shade of her umbrella and wide brimmed hat, but the costume gave her away well enough. She wore that kind of skirt that had enjoyed brief popularity before it went out of fashion somewhere in the previous decade – the kind that seemed intent to wrangle the kneecaps. He could only deduce that she went on wearing the things just to get a worthwhile return out of the effort it must have taken to learn how to walk in them. The mile-high heels were another clue. Yes, even with the sustained stare she had trained on him, there was no mistaking the lady. It was Blucille Cordon, Assistant District Attorney.

After a respectable interval passed between them, he took his hand out of the windowpane and tightened his tie back into place... and not because he wanted to look good for some social call. Her sudden appearance meant a *job*...

Just as he would have opened the door to his office, it opened for him. His momentarily befuddled gaze was met by another Mesomela lady – one he considered far more lovely. It was his own secretary, Deborah Boulevard.

"Oh, excuse me, Mr. Templar," Ms. Boulevard said in her smooth, butterscotch voice, her ubiquitous smile lighting up his gloomy office car. "I was just about to remind you of your appointment."

"*Remind* me?" he answered, incredulous, his ears settling back into a relaxed, upright posture. "I didn't have any appointment I knew about, until a moment ago." He tilted his head, giving her a questioning grin. "What tipped you off?"

She took a step into the car and brushed something off the shoulder of his suit. "Could be the fact that you fixed your tie."

He laughed once, dismissively. "You couldn't have seen me fix my tie through both our doors," he said.

She shrugged. "Well, it's not like the young lady standing by your car was any clue. After all, I couldn't see her, either."

He just shook his head. A short few years ago, Deborah had come into his employ already lauded as the greatest secretary in the world. The least he could do was let her keep a few of her trade secrets...

"My thanks, in any case," he answered. "Supposing I just sit back down and let you show the ADA in?"

Deborah turned to go back out. "That *would* be proper procedure, Boss." She shut the door between them. The door with the fine monograms...

Horus Templar – Public Defender.

* * *

Ms. Cordon stood uncomfortably in the middle of Horus' office, pouring soap into her pipe with its long, slender holder while her umbrella dripped by the doorway. Standing while he waited for her to sit, Horus watched her with equal discomfort. She was pretty young... probably only in her early thirties... and already she blew bubbles like an old miser. A stream of them floated up into the air before lazily arcing back down, and at last she seemed slightly more at ease. Then, seeming to take her first notice that they were both standing, she took the seat under the window where he had first spied her. "Sorry," she said evasively. "It was a long walk without the pipe." She blew another stream of bubbles. There was a distant look in her eyes as they searched aimlessly about his office. "I've had a lot on my mind..."

That, of course, was usual. Horus knew her well enough by now – the brilliant understudy Hamilton Blackforest was grooming to be the next District Attorney of Cape Deltrix. She was a compulsive juggler, whom he had almost never caught with her eyes on what was immediately in front of her. Her mind was always in many cases at once – her heart, in none. It was a handicap that she had a good handle on, though. Cordon had surprised him many times in court, appearing totally tuned-out, only to stymie him with a well-timed objection...

"No trouble at all," Horus reassured her. "I'm glad to see you, Ms. Cordon. Work has been a little slow for my taste."

"I don't doubt it," she replied, not looking up. "If I had as little to do as you, I think I'd develop nervous tendencies." She poured more soap.

"I'm surprised, though," he went on. "Usually, I have some advance notice of job offerings from the DA's office."

Cordon flipped a look at her pocket watch. "Your secretary keeps a good ear to the ground, I know. But this case I'm about to give you was originally going to be heard in military tribunal. The Czarina herself ordered it into the civil sector mere hours ago. She believes it is a matter of great interest to the entire country – civilians and fighting men alike."

Horus leaned eagerly over his desk. "So far, I do find myself greatly interested."

Cordon clipped her pipe into a case and took out powder and a hand-mirror, going to work on her already immaculately powdered jowls. "It's like this, Mr. Templar," she began. "A big game hunter and an exotic florist that work the skirt of the jungle found and captured an injured Dire Mantid. As a member of an insurgent state within our own borders, the creature was naturally taken prisoner by the military as a war-criminal. They were shipping him up to the Capitol – originally to face tribunal under General Schtautzi. But, as I said, he was turned over to Blackforest and the SAPD at the last minute instead, per Czarina Pretsilvi." She snapped the lid on her powder and actually looked him in the eye again. "So there you have it. I hope you don't mind being a historical figure, Templar, because this one's going to put you in the books. I don't believe anyone's ever had a bug for a client before."

Horus nodded, perhaps a bit more excited at the prospect than a professional man would want to let on. "I think I could stomach a little fame and glory, in a pinch."

"Fame, perhaps. Glory, not so much. Don't imagine the boss is going to let you win this one."

"He seldom does," Horus admitted, a flash of many pitted battles running roughshod across his brain at the mere mention of her boss. Hamilton Blackforest had been Horus' rival all through law school. Now, many years later, fate had granted both men the pleasure of challenging each other once again. In terms of courtroom brilliance, Horus felt he could hold his own. They knew each other well enough for that. But the contests now were weighted. Blackforest had the backing of the State. And states – Jast-Madiir not the least – wanted convictions. At first, Horus actually believed that could be to his advantage. He had thought prosecutors would get lazy over time – careless – so secure in the crutch that the system offered them that they couldn't help being a little off their game. But even after all these years, Blackforest hardly blinked. Worse yet, he seemed able to confer that same doggedness on all his ADAs. As Public Defender, Horus had known few enough victories, and none of them easy...

"What exactly is my client charged with?" he asked dutifully. "War crimes, yes, but that is a bit categorical. What charge, specifically?"

Cordon rifled in her handbag, as if searching for something – anything – she might need to use in it. "The highest applicable crime," she informed him. "Defamation of the Crown. And is it really any wonder? I'm sure, after all, the Czarina is not above finding it a bit embarrassing... to have gone to war with these Mantids so many times, and never have so much as a single soldier return alive. Not one. Not ever."

"Hm," Horus replied weakly, as it belatedly dawned on him just how much the Czarina might want the charges to stick. He tried not to let his ears pin themselves back.

Cordon finally settled on another look at her pocket watch. She rose quite urgently, and Horus followed suit. "If there are no questions, I think I must be going, Mr. Templar. Good day," she said, hardly giving him a breath to interject a question.

"Good day to you, Ms. Cordon," he nodded. But she had already half gone.

Even as the ADA hurried out of his office, Deborah leaned back in. "I hope you don't mind," she told him, "I just stepped out to send for Art."

Horus grinned. Artimus Mallard – his go-to private investigator. Not that Horus had any idea what he needed investigated yet... but there would be plenty of time to figure that out when he got there...

"Thank you, Deborah," he replied.

She nodded and nearly spun out to her own office car before she stopped and leaned back in. "Oh, by the way, congrats, Boss. Your name's in all of today's papers."

"*Today's papers*?" he repeated back, scratching under his chin. "You mean, the ones that won't be passed out for another couple of hours?"

She smiled her broadest. "The very same."

* * *

"She was here, wasn't she?" the great, big, burly private eye asked. He pointed admonishingly at Horus. "Don't try to tell me she wasn't. I can still smell her pipe soap."

Horus took another swig of his special morning mixture – a glass full of raw eggs – that rare providential elixir that was both invigorating and delicious. Though, the eggs were a little fresh. Things were looking up, with this new case dropped in his lap, and he always found Art Mallard to be lively company. He was of the same species as Horus, Deborah, Cordon, Blackforest... and pretty much everyone in legal professions, excluding the nation's police force, which was made up mostly of the much more common Human population. They were Mesomelae – essentially, big Jackals with upright bodies and jet-black fur. Or, mostly jet-black. Mallard had grown grey of face in the last few years, despite being still in the prime of life. Horus had never compared notes, but he suspected Mallard was actually a little younger than he was... which might account for some of his anxious tendencies. To hear Art Mallard talk, things were always just about to come unbolted on him. He had a talent for doom-and-gloom sarcasm. And, if his latest inquiry was any indication, he was a bit of a hopeless romantic...

"She was, for what it's worth," Horus answered before finishing his breakfast. "But honestly, Art, I'd try to set my sights on someone else, if I were you. All other concerns aside, you know she's bound for that job in Cape Deltrix in a few years..."

"Don't do that," Art cautioned him, getting out his bubble pipe.

"Do what?" Horus asked, almost half-innocently.

"You know very well what: Try to cut the ground out from under me, just when I might've finally found Mrs. Right. We have a lot in common, you know." He blew a long stream of bubbles.

"At least one thing in common, anyway," Horus quipped.

Art huffed. "More sarcasm. This is what I get for coming all the way over here. And just when I was about to go to sleep."

"Sleep, eh? You know I don't believe that for a second."

"Well, you should. Gosh knows even I have to catch a wink once in a while." He blew a few more bubbles and pulled up the blinds in the window beside him, wincing in the sudden light. "Just what I thought. Another bright-shiny day out. Why do you keep this office car like a cave?"

"You weren't the only one with thoughts of dabbling in sleep," Horus replied, shielding his own eyes.

Art helped himself to one of Horus' chairs, reclining as far back as he could. "Alright. I concede. You win the joshing contest for today. Now why don't you tell me about this new case of yours?"

Horus nodded, taking the seat across. "It's a bit of a doozy. Are you sure you can handle it?"

"Never. But let's have it anyway."

"Well, if you'll believe it, I'm representing a Dire Mantid charged with Defamation of the Crown."

Art stopped his bubble blowing, giving Horus a pointed stare. Then he laughed. "No wonder you're drowsy. That one must've taken you all night!"

"It's true, Art."

Mallard slowly stopped chuckling. "Really?"

"Very really."

Art studied him for a long time, finally deciding he was very, really, *truly* serious. "That *is* a doozy." He turned and stroked his white-flecked jowls thoughtfully. "What do you want me to do about it?"

"It's a little early to say," Horus admitted. "The most relevant accessories to the case, as far as I know, are the people that captured the bug in the first place – a big game hunter and an exotic florist, as I recall. I'd check with Deborah on your way out; she probably has their names, by now."

On cue, Horus' door opened, and in came Deborah. She nodded to each of them in turn. "Boss... Art."

"Hiya, toots," Art replied.

Horus shook his head. "Let me guess, you're here with the names of the hunter and the florist?"

Deborah gave him a questioning look. “I’m sure I don’t know what you mean. I was just bringing in the morning paper…”

Chapter 3

"Horus Templar to Defend Mantid," Deputy Constable Miloje read, folding open the day's news, hot off the presses. He threw the paper back down on his desk, pointing accusingly at it. "That ought to read, 'Hamilton Blackforest to *Prosecute* Mantid,'" he grumbled. "These journalists find a way to be slanted, no matter how we censure them!"

"It is a sad state of affairs, sir, I agree. What good fortune I enjoyed in Podunkville – a town too small for newsmen," Captain Alexei managed, before he blew his nose again. He looked apologetically at his superior. "Pardon the walking pneumonia, won't you?"

"Of course," Miloje nodded, his face scrunching up. "You look quite miserable, my boy, if I may say so."

Alexei went a-grin from ear to ear. "Oh, I am sir! Very much so, sir. And thank you for noticing." It was just as Miloje had guessed the night before. Captain Alexei was only too eager to show how peppy he could be while working through trauma. The Deputy Constable expected nothing less from a man who, on his own resume, had reported "exceptional pain tolerance," as his greatest character strength...

Trying not to appear too disgusted, Miloje took one last look down at the newspaper before wadding up and pitching it. "Well, enough current events. What's on my itinerary?"

The Captain adjusted his specs and produced a checklist.

"You have another meeting with Fire Chief Huizinga. He's here to discuss some of the grey areas between his jurisdiction and yours."

"Hmph," Miloje protested. *"Discuss*? More like nit-pick. The man's obsessed with establishing protocol for the most outlandish hypothetical situations you can dream of."

Alexei went on with the list. "After that, you have your interrogation with the Dire Mantid captive..."

Miloje threw himself up from his desk. "Why wait? Surely a matter of that importance ought not to be put off..."

But as he nearly stormed away, the Captain jumped in front of him. "I'm not sure they're ready for you yet, sir," he said, even as Miloje simply walked around him. "The Mantid came in injured, you'll recall..." Miloje was undeterred. "...But the local physicians were fairly beside themselves, sir, when they tried to make sense of the creature's anatomy..."

Miloje stopped in his tracks.

"They brought in the plague doctor, then?" he asked over his shoulder.

Alexei nodded. "They did, sir."

Miloje felt a slight shiver. *Of course*, he lamented. She gave him the creeps...

But, after a moment's consideration, he continued on. Facing the creepy bird-woman beat indulging the Fire Chief... if only narrowly. Very, very narrowly...

* * *

Reaching the secure door to the jail's infirmary, Miloje began to have second thoughts about rearranging his schedule. He imagined the alien bug in the dim of the cell, sprawled and drawn, being dissected and put back together – the kind of thing a Heron plague doctor probably did for fun. He could almost hear cries of agony echoing in the chamber beyond...

Waxing squeamish, he turned to leave...

"Going somewhere, Deputy Constable?"

The words, and the one standing in his way speaking them, froze him in his tracks. He looked down into the unnerving, reflective goggles of a ghastly, long-beaked mask. True to her creepiness, the plague doctor had snuck up behind him...

"Dr. Nokkaeru," he greeted her, scrambling for some composure after the sudden start. "I, erm... I thought perhaps you were already at work. I didn't want to disturb you."

"But I *am* disturbed..." she stated. "Quite regardless of what you might want."

They stood there for some time, Miloje grasping for some gracious way of ending the conversation, though of course none existed. As the awkward moment dragged on, she looked past him at the door, the leather sleeve over her long neck crinkling stiffly. He liked the look of that part of her uniform perhaps even less than the mask. It must've been something about the heavy stitching down the throat. Finally, rather than risk prolonging this uncomfortable impasse indefinitely, he resolved simply to continue by engaging her in the matter at hand. But he cleared his throat to start. There had to be *some* segue. "You were informed of the particulars, yes? Do you truly feel prepared for this strange task? It is a *Mantid* you'll be working on..."

She set down a medical case and deftly opened it to reveal a vast array of the most diabolical-looking instruments he'd ever seen or dared to have nightmares about. She paged through thick reams full of the dreadful probes until she came to a special section that actually didn't look so bad. At first glance, it was just a grid of color-coded, folded-over pieces of leather that resembled tiny little books. She plucked one out – a pretty green one – and held it out at him in her large talon. "I have everything I shall ever need to know about Mantid physiology."

Miloje eyed the micro-book with great skepticism.

"You have doubts?" she plied him.

"Forgive me, Doctor," he said, needing to be congenial. "The medical expertise of the Dire Herons is, of course, historic. But... a medical manuscript on Mantids? How could such a tome exist?"

She busied herself replacing the book and closing her case. "You forget, perhaps, that my people actually *won* our wars with the Mantid Tribes. We drove them from our island wholesale. So they are not so shrouded in mystery to us, as they are to you. We learned all about their anatomy." She seemed to take a moment of contented musing. "It is said there were many, many specimens left behind to study."

Miloje felt his pulse quicken. Again, she was being creepy. "You make your point well. Still, that was all ages ago. Surely no 'specimens' were left over for you to practice on. How can a mere book avail you, if you must perform a very involved operation on this creature? Especially such a *small* book?"

"It depends on how well the book is written," she explained. "Our volumes are intuitive, as they are condensed. They are coded in an Elfish cipher. The table of contents takes up only a quarter-inch square."

He blinked. "I am daunted, as ever, Doctor."

"Well, let us see the patient," she said, eyeing the door again. "He may die yet, if I lose too much time explaining how well equipped I come."

The Deputy Constable spun around, took up his keys and unlocked the door, holding it open. Then he tipped his bobby. "After you."

* * *

The scene was not *quite* the horror show Miloje had envisioned. It may have helped, of course, that Dr. Nokkaeru had not yet begun operating. She had retrieved her book and was rapidly making a variety of assessments with her wicked-looking calipers, fluttering back and forth between perch bars that had been installed for her on the sides of the operating table. Miloje stood transfixed by the spectacle, his face drawn back. One of their own doctors – if he'd had the knowledge – could have accomplished the same thing by quietly walking around the table, perhaps wearing a reassuring smile, using utensils that didn't look quite so much like they were intended for torture. Instead, the patient had to watch helplessly as a huge bird in dark, heavy leather performed a frightful dance over him with savagely powerful wings, sharp talons, and a bone-white mask that may as well have been the very visage of Death.

Of course, it was the sight of this patient that interested Miloje most; it was his first look at the bug out of its bag. He was immediately struck by what a pale creature it was – absolutely every bit as stark-white as the sheet draped over the table. He had heard the Mantids were supposed to be all-but invisible in the jungles they infested. Seeing one now, he was forced to dismiss that as a myth – an excuse to save face for all the generations of soldiers lost to the wars with the Tribes.

Its pale features may have been striking, but its overall form was harder to make out. It had been meticulously strapped down – they didn't dare sedate it until they knew how badly hurt it was. Mostly, he could make out that it had a very long, thin body. He almost didn't see the legs – very spindly things bound tight against the abdomen they protruded from. He had spotted them after spending a long time examining the abdomen itself. It was there he found a darker splotch that looked a bit like a big blood spot soaking through cotton bandaging. It took him too long to realize it looked like that because that was precisely what it was. The chief injury to the Mantid (or, at least, the one he had been able to spot from across the room) – was in the abdomen... but the white bandages over it had blended in so well that he hadn't discerned them from the abdomen itself.

Further up, he could see the 'business end' of the killer insect... the deadly forelegs. They were indeed much thicker and stronger than the rear legs, but didn't look so dangerous now, folded up and strapped down tight as a drum. Above that, of course, was the head – the easiest part to identify. He could see the contours of large, bulbous eye clusters and intricate muscling around the mandibles. The jaws of the Mantid were not the long, sharp caricatures he had imagined, but they looked dense and strong. They had also been left unbound... but his neck was strapped to the table well enough, so he had no appreciable reach or range of motion to try to bite with.

At the very top were a pair of antennae that were also unrestrained. The people who had improvised all these bindings had observed that the Mantid squirmed and struggled much more fiercely any time they tried to tie them down. In the end, they determined the antennae presented no threat, and just left them alone. Now, they hung in the air over the creature's head, hardly twitching. Really, the whole bug was quite motionless, as it had been since Dr. Nokkaeru began her work. It was probably much too terrified to move...

Finally, the doctor concluded her checkup, hopping down to the ground, electing to report directly to the Deputy Constable. "The patient is in no immediate danger," she said, opening her medical case at his feet again. "Your people did well to bind the wound," she went on, quickly finding what she was looking for – a tube with a canted nozzle end. "Of course, that is medicine at its most rudimentary." Holding the tube off to the side, she pulled a trigger and a jet of flame shrieked out of the nozzle. Miloje narrowly stopped himself from jumping...

"Whatever is *that* for?" he demanded.

"I will cauterize the lacerations," she explained. "But first I will have your people unwrap and clean them again, so that I may make an accurate sketch of them, before the torch further disfigures the shorn flesh."

Miloje set his jaw. "Why the sketch?"

"Do not make me do *your* job, as well as theirs," the doctor retorted, returning to the table. "Careful study of the creature's wounds may prove relevant data to his case. Particularly if the cuts are consistent with musket damage. You don't want me destroying evidence without record, do you?"

"Certainly not." Miloje was grateful, if a little stymied. "But now I must ask: how lucid is the creature? It seems... rather petrified."

The Human physicians were unwrapping the wound as Nokkaeru prepared her sketch pad. "Dire Mantids have a powerful camouflage instinct. I do not believe it is in shock, and it is not sedated. Nor do I intend that it *should be* sedated, until the blood-loss is curbed."

Miloje cleared his throat again. "You... you're going to torch the bug while it's conscious?"

"Oh yes," she said... perhaps with a bit of eagerness.

The Deputy Constable felt disinclined to be present for that. But he snapped his fingers, suddenly thinking of a way to excuse himself...

"Ah, well! If I have your assurances that the bug is lucid enough, then, I shall go retrieve the District Attorney at once! I see no reason that he and I should not take the bug's statement, when you've... er... *healed* him."

She looked back at him. "But if you go now, you will miss the procedure..."

"Just as well," he called back, already halfway out the door...

* * *

Miloje ambled his way through the DA's Office, in no hurry to retrieve Mr. Blackforest, lest he return to the infirmary too soon. He smiled and nodded at the personal secretaries of all his ADAs, hoping one of them would have something to say to him that would further slow him down. Unfortunately, they were all too busy and diligent, pausing only long enough to acknowledge him. Petty crime was up these days, as the city of St. Argonsburg steadily grew into one of the very largest in the world. Even so, Miloje and Blackforest had thus far managed to keep up with it. The SAPD prided itself in upholding the utmost efficiency. They thrived by their concise motto, which was printed on all their badges and the sides of their carriage cars: *"Arrest, Convict, Execute."*

After a brief respite to let Blackforest's secretary announce him, Miloje was shown into the DA's personal office. There were basically two modes of entering that room: either you caught Blackforest at a good time, and he would be sitting up with a big, fierce, toothy grin for you. Or, you would catch him at a busy time, and he would be hunched over a desk covered in papers, trying to wave you off with a hand of long sharp nails without bothering to look up...

"It's a busy time right now, Stenya," Blackforest growled, hunched over his desk, waving a hand up at him. "Lots of paperwork for that Mantid case. The pencil-pushers really hem me in from every side, any time a military prisoner gets turned over to civil authorities..."

Miloje took his bobby off as he worked his way deeper into the office of the top law enforcement official in all of St. Argonsburg. "It's precisely on account of the Mantid that I'm here, Hamilton."

At that, the DA looked up, a steely fire in his eyes. Blackforest was a formidable presence – not especially large as Mesomelae go, but he made up for it with his chiseled features and various sharp edges. He had razor ears that could pierce dragon flesh... a short, equally jagged fur beard... and every last one of his teeth were canines. "What about it? Don't tell me the thing died on the operating table!" The fur of his neck bristled as he looked back down at the piles of papers like he might tear them to shreds then and there, no doubt imagining he'd filled out hours' worth of forms and waivers in vain...

"No, nothing like that," Miloje assured him. "Rather, the doctor feels the creature is well enough to begin interrogation."

Blackforest's clawed fist struck the desk, sending papers flying...

"*Interrogation*!?"

Miloje didn't stop himself jumping this time. "W... well, yes... of course. That is only standard procedure."

Blackforest just glowered, one eye twitching. But slowly... unaccountably, the glimmer in his stare softened. He lazily sat back in his chair, folded his arms, and cocked his head slightly, mischief all in his smile. "You want me to watch you take a statement. From the *bug*. Is that it?" he asked through his fangs.

"Naturally," Miloje huffed. He couldn't figure what was up with Blackforest. There was nothing out of the ordinary about him coming to collect the DA for statement...

Blackforest took a belabored look at his pocket watch. "Very well. I guess I can spare a minute. Anyway, I could use a good laugh."

* * *

Miloje sat slowly with a stern expression in the seat set for him by the operating table. To his left, a typist drew his hands up over the typewriter, readying to record everything about to be said. To his right, Blackforest had resumed his relaxed, amused posture. Miloje tried not to be miffed...

"*Name*," he began... that simple one-word command that began all interrogations. He had long ago mastered saying it in a way that made most suspects crumble on the spot and spill everything...

But, to his surprise, the Mantid did not respond, or even stir. Slowly, it occurred to Miloje that, because of cultural differences, perhaps the bug didn't understand his bare-bones phraseology. "Your name, *please*, Mr. Bug..." he decided to try...

He was met with silence and stillness. The antennae bobbed in his direction for a few moments, but that was all.

Miloje shot a look over at Dr. Nokkaeru, who was still present. "You're sure this thing is awake?" he asked.

She started to cross the room in their direction. The Mantid suddenly started thrashing ineffectually against its restraints.

"Quite sure," she said.

Miloje breathed heavily through his nose and stroked his mustache. Then, he stood and leaned over the creature's face for dramatic effect – a move that honestly took a bit of steeling himself to do. It was so alien and so still. No number of restraints made him comfortable at this proximity...

"Give us your name," he said once more, infusing his voice with all the commandingness he could muster...

At last, he saw something register in the Mantid... and he knew a reply was imminent. Slowly, the mandibles opened... and finally... the creature produced a long series of chitters and clicks. Miloje's eyebrows rose. Blackforest succumbed at once to raucous laughter...

"I do hope the typist got all that," he guffawed. "*Give us your name*," he mocked. "Come on, Stenya – these things have been apart from civilization since the day they were created. Did you really think they'd be fluent in Claptrapanese?"

Miloje, fuming, did his best to ignore the DA's needling. Rather, he called on Nokkaeru again. "Well, what do you make of it, doctor? Are you perchance equipped to make heads or tails of this Mantid's speech? You did say earlier that your forebears learned all about their people..."

She shook her head. "Language is not one of the things we needed to learn in order to crush them."

The typist looked up at Miloje, aghast. "What do you want me to do, sir?"

Miloje shot him an angry look next. "Something else... far away."

"Yes, sir!" the typist agreed as he grabbed his typewriter and split.

Amid Miloje's mounting rage, Blackforest began laughing again. But before the Deputy Constable could harangue the DA for his unprofessional behavior, Blackforest spoke...

"I'm sorry... I wasn't laughing at you, Stenya. Not anymore," he chuckled. "I was just imagining the same thing playing out again... when Horus meets his client."

Chapter 4

"Well, here we are, off to meet your client," Deborah said. It was mid-morning, and she and Horus were strolling down the streets of St. Argonsburg, taking the route that led them through their preferred merchant district. The whole block was on a kind of shelf cut into the side of Mt. Norvein, as all the more modern parts of the city tended to be. They shared the stony way with all manner of commuters... peddlers, paperboys, town criers, and the obligatory guy on the corner with the sign that read, 'Onyxadon is coming.' As they neared the end of the lane, the land dropped off before them, offering a vista of The Great Harbor – the kind of view which, of course, had been very much the point of building the capitol into the flank of the mountain in the first place. More importantly, they also neared Three-Fingered Josef's Meat Market...

"Not before a bit of shopping," Horus told her, subtly changing direction toward the edge of the sidewalk.

Deborah shook her head. "You've had breakfast already. Don't you think it'd be better to pick something up on the way back?"

"The meat's not for me... as you'll soon see."

Tending the shopfront window was none other than Yuri – the proprietor of Three-Fingered Josef's, naturally. His face lit up at the sight of Horus and Deborah. For her part, Deborah got a lot of this kind of positive attention, being both famous and well-liked. Public Defenders, on the other hand, were controversial figures, and not many people in day-to-day life were so conspicuously happy to see Horus. But Yuri knew him first and foremost as one of his most valuable customers, often relieving him of merchandise that he tended to have a tough time selling otherwise...

"Hello, Yuri," Horus called to him. "What's the count of fingers down to today?"

"Still at four, Mr. Templar... still at four," Yuri replied, proudly showing his hand that was missing only the balance of the ring finger.

"You know, there are some who would say you really *are* down to three fingers," Horus joked, reaching and leaning over the counter. "If you run in the right circles, the thumb is a *digit*, not a finger."

Yuri shot furtive glances out both sides of his window. "Careful who you let hear you say that, Mr. Templar," he nearly whispered. "The Inquisitors aren't laughing about the Thumb Controversy. It's the next Indigo Heresy, I tell ya!" His expression softened. "Besides what, no matter how many fingers I've got, my name's still not *Josef*."

Horus laughed. "Aptly put."

Yuri's eyes shifted over, and he removed his hat. "And before I forget, top of the morning to you, Ms. Boulevard."

"Good morning, Yuri," she replied sweetly.

Yuri replaced his hat and looked sharply back at Horus. "And how long is it, I wonder, before I can start calling her 'Mrs.'?"

Horus' heart skipped a beat. "By high noon tomorrow, I'm sure," he joked. It was a smooth cover. The smoothest sarcastic jokes, he found, were often the ones he wished were true.

Yuri laughed, and it diffused the tension. "You two sure picked a good time to come calling! You won't believe what I found thawing in a dark, musty corner when I cleaned out the ice box the other day. Still got it sitting out where I can't smell it!"

Naturally, Horus' mouth watered with intrigue. But he was on a mission. "Not today, Yuri. I need a fresh cut."

Both Yuri and Deborah looked at him with utter stupefaction. "*Fresh*?" they asked.

"I'm afraid so," Horus admitted. "Whatever you found in the back of your ice box, it'll have to wait a while longer." He smiled. "But then, so much the better..."

* * *

Not half an hour later, they reached Civil Headquarters, and had only just enough time to check in at the front desk before they saw the lanky shape of Captain Alexei making a beeline for them. He was new to the force – or at least, to the SAPD – but already a familiar fixture. Horus winced at the sight of him, when he began to make out the man's latest disfigurements. *What has he got himself into this time*? he wondered...

"Good morning, Mr. Templar, Ms. Boulevard," the Captain called. "Welcome! We've all been watching for you. This case you're on has the whole department abuzz!"

"Good morning, Captain," Horus replied, unsure, eyeing the scratch marks all over Alexei's face.

"Pardon me a moment," Alexei said, producing a handkerchief and blowing his nose. As if the violence of his blowing action did not already seem enough to eject his brain, Horus noted that the arm holding the handkerchief was set in a cast. Alexei's pained expression reddened his grey face. When he finished, he smiled at them. "Walking pneumonia," he explained.

"Does that also account for the scars? And the arm?"

Alexei laughed. "Oh, no. Would you believe that just this morning, there was a cat up the tree, right in front of the entryway? I climbed the tree and got the cat myself!"

"More of the cat than you bargained for, it looks like," Deborah commented.

"And, the arm?" Horus plied.

"Well, I couldn't so much climb back down, once I had the cat in hand. So I jumped."

Horus blinked. "A wonder you didn't break your leg."

The Captain shrugged, looking a bit embarrassed. "Guess I didn't stick the landing just right."

"You'll have to forgive me asking," Horus put in, after a beat, "but I'm somewhat perplexed. Are you *trying* to hurt yourself?"

He nodded gleefully. "Of course! This is the big city, Mr. Templar... and I, a humble boy from Podunkville. My promotion is tenuous, at best. If I do not prove the virtue of my constitution, I shan't last long here."

Horus had to shake his head. The young man was a bit askew, but his heart was clearly in the right place. If Horus were to guess, Alexei's crime-fighting muse must've been Grand Inquisitor Enscharaulgk. He had saved the world many times by using his great body as a bulwark against evil. Of course, that approach would tend to be somewhat more effective, when one was an enormous ancient dragon...

Horus patted Alexei on the shoulder that probably wasn't hurt. "You'll get along just fine here, Alexei." He hoped. "Come now. It's high time we saw this Mantid..."

* * *

Horus' eyes narrowed as the lights came up with a flash. He stood in the midst of a dank cement bunker, built deep within the SAPD. Slowly, his sight normalized, and he scanned the wide space before him, feeling sudden anxiety. It appeared *empty*...

But at last, he noticed... something. Hardly more than a warping of the pavement, it appeared at first. But he studied it... and studied... until he could perceive something of a meaningful shape... an outline of a living creature, huddled on the ground...

"*Dianodes*," he muttered. "They really *are* invisible."

"So it turns out," Deputy Constable Miloje said, cutting in from the side of the holding cell.

Horus regarded him. "Milo," he nodded.

"Templar," Miloje replied, not bothering to tip his bobby. He tended to react to Horus with a kind of playful contempt. Horus *thought* it was playful, anyway.

They took a moment to study the Mantid, laying motionless on the other side of a huge glass barrier, before Miloje continued his earlier thought. "It was a bit of a shocker, moving the creature. When first I saw it, the thing was stark white, and I specifically thought how something that pale should have popped out of the woods like a sore thumb. But it had only changed itself to match its sheet." He looked up at Horus with a glint. "It can change to match any surroundings, Templar. Color and surface texture. It truly is the perfect killer."

Horus stroked his jowls thoughtfully, still examining his client. "Your 'perfect killer' is a little on the small side, wouldn't you say?"

Miloje hesitated. Horus wondered if that meant something. "People have been killed by smaller things," he answered.

Horus let his attention wander to the cell itself. There was, indeed, a very large sheet of glass separating the prisoner from the city officials. Above it, there was a narrow space that was open, but barred off with thick metal shafts from one wall to the other. It provided the prisoner some free range of motion (content though this one seemed to simply rest on the ground), while providing the officials an unobstructed view. Horus knew this was actually the most secure cell in the department, and used to hold the most deadly suspects. The glass was thick and strong. But exactly *how* strong was it? That was important...

"Tell me about the glass, Milo," he said.

Miloje huffed. "Suddenly sensing the danger, are we? You can trust the glass. This cell is rated to hold Avarican rogues – on their third or fourth life."

"Bulletproof?" he asked, making sure to appear quite serious.

"Easily."

Horus nodded. "Perfect."

Miloje eyed him dubiously. Then he lifted a thumb like a hitchhiker. "If you need anything, I definitely won't be behind the big, suspiciously placed mirror on the wall," he said, then turned to leave.

"Everything I need, I can get from the guards by the door," Horus replied. There were, indeed, a pair of armed guards on either side of the doorway, standing at attention with their muskets up.

Miloje didn't fidget, even if he found the response curious. He did turn to give one last parting jab as he reached the door, however. "Good luck with your interview, Templar," he said. "You'll need it."

* * *

Of course, Deputy Constable Miloje *was* behind that suspiciously placed mirror on the wall above Horus, as were Captain Alexei and Hamilton Blackforest. From the lofted vantagepoint on their side of the mirror, they could easily see and hear all that transpired in the cell below. Every embarrassing detail...

This time, Blackforest wasn't sitting back with his arms folded. He was practically on the edge of his seat, fixated on the window with predatory focus. Long-time rivals, it was little surprise how eager he was to see Horus get egg on his face. Having already been the butt of this joke earlier, Miloje certainly didn't mind seeing the shoe go to Horus' foot. Alexei, too young and naïve for such things, was pressed up against the glass. His mind was still on the wonder of the Mantid itself.

Presently, Blackforest pointed a claw at Deborah Boulevard. "She's doing it. She's setting up the typewriter." His voice was full of devious delight and he snickered. "This is going to be rich."

Miloje pursed his lips. "Don't enjoy this too much, Mr. Blackforest, or I'm liable not to enjoy it at all."

"Did you see that?!" Alexei gasped.

They both shot him an urgent stare. "See what?"

"It moved! The Mantid moved a little!"

Miloje shook his head. "I'm caught between men of extremes," he lamented to himself.

* * *

Horus took a deep breath. He steadied his nerves for the task ahead. He knew all that was about to happen was in full view of the DA and the Deputy Constable. Ordinarily, he might have wanted some client-counsel-confidentiality. But not this time. This time their eavesdropping played right into his hand...

He turned to Deborah, speaking softly. “This is going to be a little more hectic than our usual meetings with clients,” he told her. “But whatever happens, keep typing it.”

Her eyes searched him. “That *is* my job,” she reminded him, her voice betraying a bit of uncertainty. He patted her on the shoulder, then turned back to the holding cell...

* * *

“Here we go, Horus old buddy,” Hamilton said, rubbing his hands together, huge teeth clenched. “Let’s see what your client has to say for himself...”

* * *

Horus stepped up to the very edge of the glass barrier. He tapped on it with his nail...

TONK TONK TONK

The Mantid took notice. To Horus’ relief – and frankly, his amazement – it got up from the ground and unfolded itself. Standing on its four legs with its strange, slanted posture, it seemed almost smaller now than it had laying down – probably only four feet in height. Even able to make out its pinching forelegs racked with spikes and its strong mandibles, Horus still felt skeptical about the bug’s killing potential. Certainly, it seemed *possible* the thing could kill an ordinary man... perhaps not even unlikely. But the truth was just as Blucille Cordon framed it: Mantids had ended *every last trained soldier* that had ever been sent into the jungles to engage them. There was a world of difference between being able to kill, and being *that* deadly...

However, that was a point he might have occasion to examine later. Right now, he had something else to prove. And his client was no longer cooperating. It was on its feet, yes... but standing too far away. Horus needed the bug to be closer. Fortunately, he’d secured the means...

He reached into his suit jacket and retrieved the wrapped-up cut of meat from Yuri's Market, quickly removing the waxed paper covering. The Mantid's antennae, which had already been bobbing in his direction, shot up in surprise. Horus held the meat out. The Mantid was, of course, unsure. It checked around for a while, trying to feel for some kind of deception. But, eventually, it approached him...

* * *

"Wow," Captain Alexei marveled. "He's got it standing up and moving around and everything! We *definitely* never get to see anything like this in Podunkville."

Hamilton looked up from his pensive hunch. "What exactly were the sights in your little town, if I might ask?"

"For mercy's sake, don't encourage him, Hamilton," Miloje put in.

But Alexei answered with his customary pep. "Mostly dirt, sir. And sometimes plants."

"Enthralling as ever, Captain," Miloje quipped, never taking his eyes off Horus.

Blackforest homed back in as well. "I don't like it, Stenya," he said at length, while they continued to watch the Mantid cautiously close in on Horus and his little care package.

"Not much we can do," Miloje replied. "There's no civil ordinance against bribing your client. Not much precedent, either."

"It's not that," Blackforest said, gesturing out. "He's not *talking* to it! Why isn't he talking to it?"

"Could be your old nemesis was a step ahead of you, after all," Miloje said, a smile curling under his mustache. If he wasn't about to have any fun at Horus' expense, he might as well have a little at Blackforest's.

Hamilton groaned. He stood up from his seat. "I've got a mountain of paperwork to do," he said, about to leave in a huff.

"Wait," Miloje urged him. "He's clearly up to *something*. Something wily, as usual. You might as well stay and see for yourself."

The DA sighed and sat back down.

* * *

Horus finally had the Mantid right in front of him, poking its antennae against the glass where he held the meat. He smiled a kind of patronizing smile for a moment, having to remind himself that the creature was quite intelligent, and not a pet. With that thought firmly in mind, he stepped back and lobbed the meat over the glass, between the bars, so that his sentient client could enjoy a nice raw feast on the ground. It obliged him. Watching it eat, he turned more solemn. Then he stepped away...

"Excuse me, sir," he called as he approached one of the guards. The guard stood vacantly for a moment, trained to be more of a decoration than a participant in anything that ever went on in the holding cell. Finally, though, he realized Horus might actually be speaking to him. He eyed the Public Defender a few times, then gestured to himself...

"You mean *me*, Mr. Templar?" he asked.

"Yes," Horus replied. "I need something from you."

He raised an eyebrow. "I'll help if I can, sir," he said, unsure.

Horus extended his hands. "Give me your musket."

Now, the guard's eyes bugged out. "My *musket*?" He looked at his weapon in his hands, deliberating. "I... I don't know about that, sir. I'm not exactly supposed to just hand this thing out."

"I'll give it back."

The guard looked to the other guard, who gave him a shrug. Finally, he returned to Horus. "Well, alright." He handed him the musket.

"Thank you," Horus said, striding back whence he came.

* * *

"*What in the Sam Heck is he doing with that*?" Blackforest muttered.

This time, Miloje shot out of his chair, remembering the question Horus had asked...

"Stop him!" he commanded the Captain...

* * *

Horus stood before his client again. He tapped on the glass again, too... just as before...

TONK TONK TONK

The Mantid looked up, anticipant. It returned to him...

Slowly, Horus leveled the weapon directly at his client. However much their jobs might put them at odds, he trusted Miloje's word enough to do what he was about to do. But he couldn't help being a bit double-minded, even so. There was a weight on his heart as he watched the Mantid examine the bayonet end with its antennae, much as it had the meat...

Horus aimed down the sights...

BANG!!!

The Mantid threw itself back shrieking from the glass, wing-covers opening up on its abdomen. It cowered and chittered where it landed. Horus sighed, resting the stock of the musket against the ground as he looked on with shame and pity. The Mantid, of course, was unhurt. The bullet had merely left a scratch on the glass. But he hated to so betray someone's trust. Especially a client's...

After a moment had passed between him and the terrified insect, he turned, ready to relinquish the weapon to the guard. The guard, for his part, was very eager to have it back. Even as he was snatching it away from Horus, Captain Alexei entered the room...

"Say, now! What is the meaning of this?!" he demanded.

"Sorry for the disturbance," Horus replied. "No doubt I caused a bit of mischief. Perhaps I ought to clear myself with the DA and the Deputy Constable?" he asked, shooting a look up at the mirror, knowing they were looking back down at him.

Alexei blinked and stammered... and fell silent. It was a highly unusual situation, which made it hard to react right away, even with Horus essentially telling him exactly what to do. Perhaps *especially*...

"Well, come on then..." the Captain huffed at length. Horus went to follow, but stopped by his secretary...

"Did you get all that?" he asked.

"Of course," she reassured him.

He nodded, then fell in step behind the Captain.

* * *

"You do have a penchant for the outrageous," Blackforest fumed, pacing the room, illumined only by the desk lamp that hung in Horus' face. "But this time, you've outdone yourself, Horus." He spun and glowered. "Mind telling me what would possess a defense attorney to shoot his own client?"

"I think you know," Horus said, unintimidated as he sat, powerful law enforcers circling him. "Furthermore, I submit that you're morally obligated to throw this case out, at once. To go forward with it now would be a sham."

Miloje leaned over the desk, taking his turn in the interrogation. "Evasion and insinuation aren't going to look good on the incident report," he cautioned. "*Why*, Counselor? Why the stunt with the gun?"

Horus breathed through his nose, absently adjusting his cufflinks. "Well, for starters, I couldn't very well *talk* with my new client, could I?"

Blackforest and Miloje exchanged a look. "No," Miloje admitted. "Not unless you know bug-speak."

"Regrettably, I don't. That limited my options, as you might imagine – not being able to learn my client's name, or even where in the jungle he hails from. So, I dreamed up this experiment. Present the creature with a musket – the very weapon our soldiers would have brought with them into the jungle. In the last war, and the war before that, stretching back generations. And, if it had reacted fearfully to having the barrel leveled in its face, I would have to submit it was plausible the creature has seen some of that warfare." He looked up accusingly at Miloje. "But it is patently obvious from his reaction that the bug has never seen a musket before in his life."

Miloje shook his head. "Not so fast, Templar," he challenged, shifting his weight. "You're drawing conclusions. You didn't necessarily prove that he's never seen a musket. Suppose the soldier carrying one simply never got a chance to use it. You said so yourself: They're *invisible*. Ambush fighters, Templar! If our success rate against them is any indication, I doubt very much they ever give our boys the opportunity to fight back."

Horus looked past him to Blackforest, whose eyes were trained away in thought. "Is that your position on this, Hamilton?"

"That's the *State's* position," he said contemplatively, rolling his fingers under his tight pharaoh beard.

Horus was rather disappointed, if not surprised. He stood. "Very well. My client remains in your custody... for now. What about me? Are you planning on holding me liable for something?"

They exchanged glances again.

"You may go, Counselor," Miloje grumbled. "But please, in the future, show a bit more respect for state property. And our blood pressure."

* * *

"Well, that was memorable," Deborah said, the two of them making their return trip from the station.

"It was destructive," Horus lamented. "A stunt like that would have been worth it if I'd got him off then and there. Now I'll need him to trust me again. But I doubt if any amount of meat will get me back to where we started."

"Being able to talk to him would certainly help."

He grunted. "It certainly wouldn't hurt. Too bad it's impossible."

"Nothing's impossible, Boss."

He stopped in his tracks. "You have a lead?"

She seemed to curse herself. "I shouldn't have said anything."

"Au contraire! Say more."

She scratched behind one of her ears. "I know I read something in the paper once about a Meduseldan linguist who was studying the Mantid Tribes. Oh, but that was ages ago! I don't know what ever came of it."

Horus was taken aback. Not by his secretary's ability to recall obscure headlines from antiquity; that was normal. Rather, he was struck by the idea of the Meduseldan linguist. It was perfect, really... and it didn't take long to realize why. Meduselda were a peculiar species, to say the least – something the Creators had dreamt up just as they were getting started making the universe. As an early draft of life-form, they had all kinds of quirks. They didn't have hearts, lungs, spleens... a single organ to speak of... or even a head. They didn't eat, drink, sleep, or breathe. They just floated around, like glowing, airborne jellyfish. But perhaps the oddest – and most important – difference between themselves and all other forms of life was this: They always lived to be a hundred and forty years old. Every single one of them, no matter what – with only the notable exception of the Queens, who lived much longer. *If* they were killed before that – whether once, a hundred, or even a zillion times – they'd just spend a week in a ghostly form, and then harden back to normal. Thus, there was really no reason a Meduseldan couldn't simply float out into the woods and pester a Mantid Tribe all he wanted. They'd kill him, of course. They'd kill him until they got tired of it. And after that he could study in peace...

"Deborah, that's an incredible lead! Why, short of announcing you had the Rosacea Stone in your back pocket, I can't imagine a better chance at getting by the language barrier." He cocked his head at her. "You really would have left that unmentioned?"

"Only until I had a chance to look into it myself. I didn't want to get your hopes up."

He smiled. "Very considerate. Planning a trip to the local Dronehood office, are we?" He spoke of the Clerical Dronehood of Berlberi – an international confederation of data enthusiasts, owned and operated, incidentally enough, by the aforementioned Meduselda. Their people may not have had much of a handle on the spice of life... but they certainly loved their paperwork. They would have record of the linguist, unquestionably. It would simply be a matter of sifting through the records they kept of *absolutely everything* to find it...

"That's where I'll be for the rest of the day, I expect," she answered. "Unless you have something more important for me to do."

"I'm sure I don't," he said. Then he remembered something, snapping his fingers. "In all the excitement, I forgot to mine Hamilton's papers."

She produced a thick stack from her typewriter bag. "I got photostats during your interrogation."

He took them from her with a grin, scanning through. "Sparse list of witnesses. Hardly any surprise." He blinked once, noticing a name printed twice. Blackforest seldom erred, so such a typo was surprising. Nevertheless, he continued on. "How do you think Art is coming along, finding the folks who brought in the Mantid?"

She shrugged. "If he had any trouble, I think he would have found *us* by now. He might be talking to them as we speak."

"Let's hope so. We may need him back soon, to chase *your* lead."

She put her hand on her hip. "And suppose my lead sends him off on safari? I'm telling you Boss, don't stake everything on this linguist thing just yet. You've sent Art on some wild misadventures before, but I doubt even *you* can talk him into jungles full of Mantids."

"Not without a fair bit of complaining on his part, at any rate. We'll have to hope it doesn't come to that." His ears perked. "Fortunately, if I'm very successful with my next call, he'll be off the hook."

"Where exactly are *you* going, then?"

"To see if I can get this case thrown out before it even starts."

She shook her head. "You just tried that with Blackforest. It didn't work. Who are you going to appeal to? The Czarina herself?"

Now, he shook *his* head. "Someone higher than that."

Chapter 5

The shadows lengthened and the sky filled with bands of color as the sun and Phantom Light waned in the dusk. Art Mallard had whiled the day riding around to the south side of Mt. Norvein – a journey that had taken him by train and carriage. He was a seasoned traveler, chasing leads wherever they took him. Even so, a long day spent as a passenger – particularly in a carriage on a stony trail – tended to take a toll on his backside. Enjoying one last blow of his pipe as the horse and buggy neared town, Art reminded himself to be thankful he didn't have a tail. He very well *might* have, after all, if the Creators had remolded his species out of traditional jackals only slightly differently. As it was, there was broad approval among Mesomelae that their Makers had left that feature out – and not just because they probably would have made sitting in most chairs even more uncomfortable. Rather, Mesomelae liked to cultivate an image of sophistication and refinement. And it was certainly more refined to express your feelings with your face than with your butt.

At last, the carriage came to a halt. Art needed to hop-to-it before curfew, so he flipped the carriage driver a big coin. "Keep the change, ma'am," he said.

She looked at the coin with bugged eyes, shaking her head. "Oh, no! I'm afraid I can't do that, mister. One more discrepancy on my annual income audit, and I'll be executed!"

Art sighed. There were a lot of reasons to execute somebody, and the Czars and Czarinas of Jast-Madiir must've thought of nearly every one of them by now. Begrudgingly, he fumbled around in his money pouch for a bunch of smaller coins...

* * *

Standing under a streetlamp, hands tucked in the pockets of his trench coat, Art Mallard studied the building ahead of him, eyes narrow beneath his brimmed hat. Being a private eye required many different things: a keen eye, a sharp mind, brawn, stealth, a lot of luck... and self-imposed chronic insomnia. And if all that wasn't enough, it was also important to dress for success. Sometimes, you could get the job done with just the trench coat. But it certainly never hurt to wear the hat...

Art took little time convincing himself that this was the inn he was looking for. For one thing, it was the inn that was swarming with police. For another, it was the only inn in town. Tossing an empty soap bottle into a nearby trash can, he made his way nonchalantly up to the front door...

As he strode, he reviewed what he knew. He was looking for two Humans – a man and his wife – a big game hunter and an exotic florist – the ones who had found the Mantid in the jungle and brought it in to the local authorities. They were being transported by the police to St. Argonsburg, so that they could be present for the trial, in case they needed to appear as material witnesses. Aside from the bug's police and military handlers, these two were practically the only people of interest yet in the case...

After that, the details got a little more perplexing. The man went by the name "Mich" Monroe. His wife, curiously, also went by the name "Mich" Monroe. Since all Human marriages were strictly by arrangement, the two having some cute story about how they shared lifelong nicknames clearly had no bearing on their association. Even stranger, individuals of every species only had one birthname. The only people with last names were those who bought one from the state – and the state chose the name for you at random. The fact that these two people had not one, but *two* matching names defied all the astronomical possibilities. Art knew, of course, that this matter of coincidence probably meant nothing to his investigation whatsoever. But he would have to ask about it anyway, if only to stop himself being too distracted by how weird it was...

"Hold there," a policeman called out, pointing with a nightstick. "Are you here to speak with the witnesses we're transporting?"

This was a critical juncture. Art Mallard was indeed consummate at stealth, and could easily have slipped by the cops unnoticed if he'd wished. Some time ago, he had perfected the art of perfect inconspicuousness. All it really took was a newspaper to hold up in front of his face. But that was a skill he didn't want to abuse... and anyway, if the cops happened to overhear him talking to the witnesses after slipping past them, he'd have some uncomfortable explaining to do. Rather, he decided to be up front with them. And now, he was at their mercy. The next thing to come out of his mouth was crucial. In order to have any chance at all of talking with the Monroes, Art would have to answer the policeman's question with just the right discretion and phraseology...

"Yup," he said.

The cop nodded. "Well alright, then. Right this way..."

* * *

At their prompting, Art helped himself to a nice, cushiony chair. Sharing a couch across from him was a big, stout man in overalls and a petite woman in a dress with frilly shoulders – and a bandage around one of her forearms. The 'Miches' Monroe. A tense, breathless mood – and just a whiff of aloe – hung in the air. Art took out a notepad, ready to get their stories... starting, of course, with that annoying bit about names...

"Your birthname, ma'am? The *full* name, if you please..."

She bit her lip, searching her husband's face before answering. Huddled together, both of the Monroes were ill at ease – like they were trying to brace each other through some sort of ordeal. There could be a nuance difference, of course, between a couple seated close out of mere affection, and one doing so for the sake of mutual strength. But this time it wasn't even subtle. These people weren't experienced liars. And they were hiding something...

"Michelle," the woman answered.

"And you?"

"Mitchel," the man answered.

Art nodded as he jotted that down. It matched his guess well enough, though he'd thought perhaps the man's name was Michael. Still, there was that other part...

"And... the matching last names?"

"Pure coincidence," Mitchel answered.

"The irony is, we bought them so people could finally tell us apart," Michelle continued.

"I see." Art accepted the answers with little hesitance. He was pretty sure they hadn't lied. Not yet. But what *were* they hiding? The only way to find out what was to keep going...

He looked at the man. "What was it you were out hunting, the day you found the Mantid?"

"Moose, leopard, dilophosaur..." Michelle answered in his stead. "Whatever comes by. There haven't been any commissions for trophy animals in a while. But big game hunting is a *job*. If a big game hunter is caught not hunting, that means dereliction of duty... and execution."

"Alright," Art assented, looking at Michelle now. "And how about the exotic florist work?"

"Just a fancy term for going out into the jungle to scavenge for scorch dandelions," Mitchel answered. "Technically, they're not even flowers, you know. They're weeds. But very valuable weeds – they're the only known plants in the world that are constantly on fire – and they only grow deep in Jast-Madiir's jungles."

From this, Art put one little piece of the puzzle together. Although, really, all he'd done was recognize a hasty assumption he'd made...

"Let me guess," he said, pointing his pen at Mitchel. "You're the florist."

"That's right."

He shifted his pen to Michelle. "And you're the big game hunter?"

She shrugged. "That's how conscription goes sometimes."

"Uh-huh," Art said, returning to his notepad. "So tell me about that morning. About finding the Mantid. How did that go down? Who saw him first?"

They looked at each other again. Art was, of course, quite professionally accustomed to the suspense of mystery. Even so, wondering where their deception came in was beginning to wear on him. But when Michelle began to itch at the bandage on her arm... and he got another whiff of aloe... he began to form a theory...

"I found the Mantid," Michelle answered. "I nearly stepped on it... it was hidden so well. But it was hurt badly. I thought it was dead at first... or else asleep. But mostly it was lethargic from blood loss. I bandaged it, and I fed it. Then I went to find my husband."

"You can appreciate my surprise at what she found," Mitchel continued. "We were both pretty shocked. Sure, when we'd first started our jobs in the jungle, we thought about Mantids all the time. Figured one day we'd run afoul of them, and we'd be history. But after the first few years of coming back home alive every night, we mostly forgot about them. Decided they must live a bit deeper in. To find one – and not have it eat us – that was the last thing we expected."

"How about getting it out of the woods?"

Mitchel laughed nervously. "I've helped Michelle lug a lot heavier things out in her day. Once we had the bug tied up, carrying him was no trouble."

Finally, Art pointed at the bandage on Michelle's arm. "And, finding the bug... that's how you got *that*?"

Here, she hesitated. "Yes," she nodded, not making eye contact. Art let the silence hang, until her discomfort obliged her to expound further. "It... it took a swipe at me."

"Sure it did," Art said, closing his notebook. He stood up. "Care if I take a sniff of that bandage, ma'am?"

Her eyebrows fidgeted at the strange question. "I guess not."

She slowly held out her wrist. Mallard smelled it with his finely tuned snout. "Just what I thought," he said. "*Aloe*. You know what aloe is used for, Miss? I think maybe you do. It's not for cuts. It's for treating *burns*." He sat back down, adjusting his coat. "Frankly, lady, I don't believe the bug swiped at you. I have a different theory about your injury altogether." He leaned forward in his seat. "But suppose I give you guys another chance to tell me the truth. The *real* truth."

They looked at each other once again – and this time, Art knew, they had reached unspoken consensus to actually spill the beans...

"Promise you won't share this with anyone but your defense lawyer," Mitchel urged him.

"Scout's honor," Art replied.

"We... that is..." Michelle began. "We switch jobs... sometimes."

Art sighed. "Yeah. That's what I thought."

"It seemed harmless enough at first," Mitchel explained. "We'd both go into the woods, and we'd come back out with scorch dandelions and big dead animals. Same as always. We figured, what did it matter, which of us got what, so long as we came back with the proper haul?" He shrugged. "The flower business ain't so bad, Mr. Mallard. But sometimes, a man just wants to go out and shoot something with his own two hands, you know?"

"And I like to pick flowers once in a while," Michelle agreed. "Although, I'd like it better yet if they weren't such a fire hazard."

"But you *were* the one who found the Mantid?" Art asked her.

She nodded. "Yes, that part was no lie. I stood there so stunned, I accidentally burned myself on the flowers I'd rounded up."

"But you had to change your story, so it wouldn't be found out you were the one collecting the dandelions that day?"

They both nodded. "If it's discovered by the authorities that we weren't doing our jobs, it'll be the death penalty," Mitchel said.

Art let out a very long breath through his nose, stroking his whiskers. "This is a pickle," he lamented. "I suppose you told the cops the same story about the bandage you told me?"

"I did."

He shook his head. "This is a pickle of a pickle. The bug's only possible defense, as far as I can tell, is for Horus Templar to try to convince the jury that he has no history of violence toward Humans. That makes you two his most valuable defense witnesses. He didn't hurt you, even when he was unbound. But you can't change your story, since that'll shed suspicion on your injury. Then they might find out about your job-swap..."

"Please, Mr. Mallard, don't call on us as defense witnesses," Mitchel implored him. "It'll almost surely mean we get executed."

Michelle agreed. "Especially if we get charged with perjury to boot. Then we'll be *double* executed!"

"You can't be charged with perjury, unless you first swear in court under oath and then repeat your lie. But I have to admit, Blackforest will more than likely bring you forward to do just that." He paused sullenly. "Either way, I don't see how Horus can use you to help the bug without putting you on the chopping block."

"Do you think he'd do that?" Michelle asked.

Art shook his head. "No. Not Horus." They showed palpable relief. "But that leaves us still in an awful bind."

"We're so sorry for your lawyer friend and his client, Mr. Mallard," Michelle said. "If there's anything else we can do..."

"Only one thing I can think of right now," Art said, standing to go. "Next time, don't lie. Just wear sleeves."

Chapter 6

Having only just come from Civil HQ, Horus found himself opposite an austere monument to social order of a different kind. He crossed a drawbridge over a deep, barren moat. He passed right by hulking, reptilian specimens shrouded under dark hoods, inscrutable masks, and other layers of mystery – each larger and stronger than he, cradling a huge gun – frozen in motionless vigil. He reached their stark fortress of metal, a pair of guards obliging him without a word, opening monolithic doors. Standing just on the other side was another Avarican, whose drapery reached all the way to the floor.

"Greetings," she began with a slight nod, her gaunt but elegant hands joined before her. "Please state your name and business."

"Horus Templar," he said, nodding in return. "I'm a Public Defender for the city of St. Argonsburg. I was hoping I could set up an appointment to speak with one of your emissaries." He cleared his throat, hesitating. "My apologies – I spent the whole trip trying to decide exactly what to say for myself when I arrived... but this is a rather unusual matter. I have a client – shall we say – of a foreign persuasion."

"Say no more, Mr. Templar," the Door Keeper said, raising a hand. "You represent the Dire Mantid. We are apprised of this matter. Even so, the Inquisition thanks you for searching us out of your own accord. Rare indeed is the one who is so forthright with our Order. Why that is, I could not say."

"I can't imagine."

The Door Keeper turned, gesturing for him to fall in step as she led him deeper into the echoing outpost. "I regret that it is not within my power to grant you proper audience at present. But I shall show you where you may be accommodated, as we await the return of Primary Administrator Hihvnor."

Horus blanched. "A Primary Administrator?" he marveled aloud. "I'm... I'm rather overwhelmed to be offered the ear of someone so elevated." It *was* a rather overwhelming thought. Though the gulf was wide, Primary Administrators were second only in importance to the Grand Inquisitors themselves. But truly, this exceeded his wildest hopes. Such an Administrator might carry enough weight by himself to get Horus' client off the hook, if his negotiations were successful...

"I am sure Hihvnor will be most pleased to treat with you directly. He may be a Primary Administrator, but he is first and foremost an envoy. Grand Inquisitor Netrinemo sent him to the Archipelago many years ago to coordinate our outreach to the Mantid Tribes. Thus, the matter of your client is of paramount concern to him." She stopped mid-step, turning to him. "However, I would caution you to refrain from further awe at his high station, when the two of you meet. We Inquisitors work quite diligently to pride ourselves in our humility."

Horus nodded his agreement. "Understood." Involuntarily, his ears turned back a bit. "When are you expecting Hihvnor to return?" In the company of such ascetic folk, Horus began to worry they might ask him to stay and wait for days and not think anything of it...

"He will return by the stroke of fourteen," she explained. Horus was relieved. That was less than two hours out...

"Wonderful," he said. "My office will be out of town longer than that, anyway."

"I am only sorry the Administrator is unable to see you at once. These are demanding times. But you may wait for him in his office."

"His *office*? Is that usual? Isn't there a guest lobby, or something...?"

"Hihvnor will not mind. And I can think of no better place to put you up, until he arrives. His office boasts our most lavish accommodations."

* * *

Soon enough, Horus was admiring the luxuries of Hihvnor's office for himself. There was a bed, a desk, two chairs, a lamp, a wardrobe, an armory chest, and a wash basin. The only features besides that – the ones that must have been 'lavish' – were a window and a small personal library – a predictable but sturdy canon of Shaikkonen's *Ascetic Disciplines* and several volumes of Magormissahr's *Referendums on the World*. Horus was used to letting long hours slip by between meaningful bursts of work, but he whiled the time rather anxiously in that office. It didn't help that his chair was very uncomfortable – probably designed that way on purpose, for sake of penance. He was just about to pick up a *Referendum* when he heard heavy footfalls in the corridor...

Suddenly, the office door opened, and in walked the one who must have been Hihvnor. Horus regretted he didn't know how Inquisitors' uniforms differed to show rank. If Hihvnor had been a General in some army, he would've been decked in fancy, shiny medals. But this was the Inquisition. He wore simple cloth. The only metal accoutrements on him were his mask, his buttons, his sidearm, and his ankle weights...

"Hello, Mr. Templar!" Hihvnor said, perhaps as exuberant as any Inquisitor allowed himself to be. "I am so sorry to keep you waiting."

Horus grinned, knowing Hihvnor had arrived well ahead of the Door Keeper's estimate. "Nice to meet you, Administrator. No need to excuse yourself – you're still early by my reckoning."

"In my line of work, it is impossible to be early," he said, gesturing for Horus to sit again, as he rested a hand on the back of his own desk chair. "What a curious circumstance that has prompted this meeting! I have studied the known history of the Tribes, and this is indeed unprecedented. Even the Herons who came to settle Roemnar never took a living captive. Those who did not escape that island fought and died to the last insect."

Horus – an observant sort – could hardly help noticing an unaddressed gash on Hihvnor's shoulder. "Looks like you've been in a scuffle yourself, recently."

Hihvnor craned his head around on the long neck he had coiled beneath his hood, searching for the wound Horus indicated. "I was detained by rather unpleasant work, yes. Another aggressive Digit Cult we had to disband. We've broken up dozens in St. Argonsburg alone over the last few months."

Horus blinked. Yuri's word of caution about the Thumb Controversy was more informed than he'd guessed. "That's rather shocking. Are they all so... '*unpleasant*'?"

Hihvnor shook his head. "Oh, no. Most heretics profess proper thumb-as-finger doctrine with only token urging, and accept the dunce cap. But a few are more violently zealous, as you see."

Horus nodded, waxing solemn. "All the more I thank you for seeing me on such short notice. I'm at an impasse with this case already. I all-but proved the Mantid's ignorance of Human warfare earlier today... but even so, I failed to impress the District Attorney. It doesn't appear that there's much hope of defending the creature, if I can't prevent his case from reaching court. It's just too sensational – the Czarina's first opportunity to avenge herself on the infamous bugs that have been getting the best of her and her family for ages." He gave Hihvnor a purposeful look. "That's why I hoped to appeal to you... to the Inquisition, that is. You've pardoned capital crimes before... and I believe it's in your best interest to do so here. Think of it, Hihvnor. Think of what you could learn if the Mantid was turned over to you. You might finally discover a peaceful way to open a dialogue with the Tribes."

There was a brief moment of silent consideration. Hihvnor's head drooped on his neck. Horus' heart drooped with it...

"I fear what you ask may not be possible, Mr. Templar," he lamented. "It is the business of the Grand Inquisitors alone to grant the pardon that you seek. Our chapter in the Archipelago has been regrettably out of contact with the continent for some time. Enscharaulgk, I think, would grant your request... if he could. But you know how *he* is."

Horus nodded. "Dead."

"Precisely. And so he may remain for some time." At this juncture, Hihvnor rounded the desk, and set an affirming, scaly hand on Horus' shoulder. "Rest assured, my friend, that I have already sought what you ask, even so. Dispatches were sent to all the Primary Administrators within hours of our learning of the Mantid captive. I petitioned my fellows for the authority to grant Enscharaulgk's pardon in his stead. They can, by consensus, confer on me that power, if they choose."

"But you have doubts?"

Hihvnor sighed, and Horus could feel the heat stoked in his breath. "I fear some will not see just cause. The Grand Inquisitors firmly established the precedent of granting pardon where noble deeds outweighed state crimes. If this Mantid has done anything noble, then neither you nor I can swear to it. We have no way of knowing. The Administrators will see, as I do, that I am only begging this pardon in the hopes of advancing one of our own interests."

Horus shook his head. "Well, if it helps, you could inform the other Administrators that they'd also be advancing *my* interests."

Hihvnor chuckled – a response that almost floored Horus. "We'll see what they decide. Their assent is possible. But your hopes should not depend on it. Rather, I suspect my hopes will depend on *your* defense. I wish you good fortune, Mr. Templar. The Inquisition wishes you good fortune."

Horus rose to go, and the two shook hands. "Thank you, Hihvnor. Good luck with those pesky Digit Cults."

* * *

Taking his leave of the Inquisition Outpost, Hihvnor's personable demeanor didn't prop Horus' spirits up for long. The errand, in any case, had been another futile one. It would have been better, he reckoned, to have not even thought of appealing to the Inquisitors. Then, perhaps, they might have surprised him by pulling the case out from under Blackforest at the last minute – unlikely as that was. Now, he would have to try not to be too distracted by his hopes that they could still pull it off. Despite Hihvnor's reservations, he was more likely to succeed than Horus was, at present. Deborah would find out about the linguist, he was sure... but it seemed a long shot they could reach him, let alone in time... and even knowing the bug's language might not help. Horus was just going to have to hope that Art had got something useful...

Chapter 7

"I didn't get anything useful from the Monroes," Art Mallard said.

Horus set down his dinner fork – carefully, so his malaise didn't show. Art had travelled all morning and joined them just in time for brunch, apparently only to convey that his errand had been futile. Nothing they'd tried or investigated so far was yielding very hopeful results. It was enough that Horus began to lose his appetite.

"You'll have to be more specific than that, Art," Horus said, dabbing his face with his napkin. "What were the useless things you learned? Did you basically corroborate the statement they gave the police?"

Art huffed. "Hardly. The bug didn't even fight back when they found it. Maybe feeding and bandaging it was enough to gain its trust. But in any case it was probably too weak to give them much trouble."

Horus gave him a puzzled look. "Well, that certainly *doesn't* match their statement. If I can get them to admit as much, it will be harder for Hamilton to paint the Mantid as a hardened enemy of the state. How is that not useful?"

"Because you can't call them on their lie, Horus. You won't want to." Whatever point Art was driving at was getting to him, and he went for his soap bottle...

"Ah-ah," Deborah stopped him up. "You know the house rules. No bubbles at the table."

Art sighed, putting the bottle back into the deep vest pocket of his trench coat.

"I suppose Hamilton *will* call them first," Horus went on musing. "You're worried they'll be liable for perjury?"

"It goes well beyond that." Art eyed Horus solemnly. "They job-swapped, Horus. Now they're scared stiff it'll be found out. If the lady's injury is called into question, it *will* be."

Horus ran a hand over his pinned-back ears, letting out a long, labored breath. "That is unfortunate," he managed. "But I guess it makes little difference what the bug did when he was picked up, either way."

"How do you figure?"

"Well, how would you read this case, Art? Do you think the Czarina means to put *this* Mantid on trial, or *all* Mantids? I fear this is a symbolic reckoning, not a true criminal case. It won't matter that the state can't prove this Mantid ever served in war against us. All that matters is, we can't prove he didn't."

Art finished a morsel of meat. "Sunshine and roses, as usual. Anyway, that was my day. How did you fill the time, after your little visit to the SAPD?" By this time, they'd already discussed Horus' eventful meeting with his client.

"Would you believe I paid a visit to a Primary Administrator?"

Art stopped short of taking another bite. "You mean, one of those Inquisitor big-wigs?"

"Yes."

The P.I. looked aghast. "You were in there with all the scary lizards, talking to one of their head honchos?"

Horus managed a chuckle. "They are formidable, I grant, but equally disciplined. And the rules they live and work by are simple and sturdy. It never occurred to me to think of Inquisitors as 'scary'."

Deborah beamed at Art sarcastically. "Most people don't... unless they have something to hide."

"Darn right I do," Art replied. "Like a real nice new fishing boat, for starters."

Horus laughed a bit more openly. "Now when would you ever find time to fish?"

"You let me worry about that. The main thing is, if I ever do, I'll have a swanky boat already waiting for me." He shook his head dismissively. "I'm just glad you didn't send me on that particular expedition."

Now Deborah set down her dinner fork, as she and Horus exchanged a look. Art noticed their silent council, abandoning his bite of meat again. He shot glances at them both. "Alright, where *do* you have me going next? Looks like I'm the only one who doesn't know."

Horus folded his hands. "Our dear Deborah did unearth *one* lead worthy of following up on yesterday."

"Swell," Art said, intuiting well enough that they were about to take the long way around to explain a monumental bit of sleuthing they expected him to do. "Let's have all the details."

"Well, of course, I'm sure you can appreciate how much it would help if I could actually *speak* with my client."

"It doesn't exactly strain the limits of my imagination." Art began fidgeting as his nerves wore on him. "But what do you want *me* to do about it? Live among the Tribes as a jungle castaway for a few years, slowly learning their language?"

"Unfortunately, we don't have that kind of time," Horus replied. "The trial begins in three weeks. We need to find someone who already knows their speech."

"Is there such a person?"

"There is," Deborah put in. "A Meduseldan linguist."

Art stroked his whiskers thoughtfully. "Come to think of it, I do recall reading about something like that in the papers a few years back."

"So did Deborah," Horus explained. "She spent the day at the local Dronehood office, seeing what she could dig up on him."

Art huffed. "That must've been a job."

"You wouldn't know it, to watch the Clerks," Deborah replied. "You should have seen them light up when I told them what I was looking for... a minor news story from an indeterminate number of years ago."

Art chuckled. "I bet the jellies probably had old newspapers stacked to the sky in no time."

"Oh, they had to sift through a lot more than just newspapers," Deborah said, shaking her head. "Evidently you don't know the Berlberi filing system. Every record and paper of interest gets filed in the same cabinets, in the order they receive it. Birth certificates, death records, survey templates, public announcements, royal decrees – I even found a comparative statistical report on the number of spoons per capita for all the burbs of St. Argonsburg."

"You mean you *participated* in that hunt for a needle in a needle stack?" Art said, ears rigid with incredulity.

Deborah shrugged. "Let's just say I tried to help. But honestly I got the feeling I was only slowing them down." She shook her head again with a vacant look. "Those Meduselda and their papers. I ought to thank my lucky stars the Dronehood doesn't shop its members out as secretaries. If they ever did, all my fame would go right out the window."

"You'd still be a winner in our book, sweetheart," Art winked. "But anyway, what about this linguist? No doubt they found something on him..."

"They did. First the article, then they went on another merry hunt for anything else they could find." Deborah reached under the table and produced a bunch of documents. "Here's what they found. When it was all through, they were eager to know if I had anything else really obscure they could look up for me. I hated to hurt their feelings and admit I didn't."

"Well, never mind *their* feelings," Art said. "What about little old me? I'm still in suspense wondering where in the world this linguist is, and why you both seem to anticipate an ordeal."

Horus cleared his throat. "Yes, well, that is the rub. He's not strictly local, at present. Recently he's moved on from his studies of the Jast-Madiir Tribes, in favor of more distant jungles."

Art briefly hesitated before venturing his guess. "Maenean jungles, I presume?"

Horus nodded solemnly. "I'm afraid so."

"Hot dog," Art sighed, starting to rap his claws on the table. "Now I really need a puff." It was rather ominous news. Maenea was not the easiest country to travel to at the moment. The Czarina had initiated a trade war with their northern neighbor a few months prior. The situation had since deteriorated to the very brink of *actual* war, where it had been tensely hanging by a thread for the last several weeks. Everyone in St. Argonsburg expected to hear tell of opening volleys from one naval blockade or other any day now. No doubt, Art would prefer to read about it in the papers, rather than experience such things firsthand. Even if the journey to Maenea was uneventful, the return trip would present equal danger. To say nothing of what the actual job of locating the linguist would entail...

"So, let's say I can make it to Maenea and back without getting blown out of the water," Art began.

"I would like to believe it's possible," Horus quipped.

"Wouldn't we all? But even if it is, how do I get in contact with this... what did you say his name was?"

"Jojojo," Deborah said.

Art looked incredulous. "*Jojojo*? You mean like, 'J-O-J-O-J-O'?"

"That's how it's spelled," she shrugged.

He shook his head at her. "Well, how do you know it isn't pronounced 'Yo-yo-yo'? Or 'Ho-ho-ho'? J's can be tricky that way, you know."

She waved off the comment. "You got me, Art. I guess it could be any one of them. But honestly, I'd say that's the least of your worries."

"Right," Art nodded. "As I *did* begin to say, even supposing I slip both blockades, how am I even supposed to find 'Joe Translator'? Knowing what country he's in is one thing. A very small thing, at that. Do you want me to go wandering in the woods, politely asking all the killer bugs which way the round glowy fellow went?"

Horus gave him a weak grin. “I’m afraid that’s in your court. You *are* the private investigator. I daresay if anyone could figure out how to get in touch with an unreachable, unfindable linguist, it would be you.” He stood from the table, giving Art a pat on the shoulder. “Think on it, Art. Think as if your life depended on it.”

“Which, of course, it does.”

“All the more reason I’m sure you’ll come up with something clever.”

Deborah stood from the table too, reaching to collect all the half-picked-over plates. Art looked up at them both. “That’s it then, huh?” he asked. “Some farewell I get. *‘Here’s your hat, where’s your hurry’*?”

“Well, time is a-wasting,” Horus said, helping with the dishes. “That shooting war could start any moment. Probably best you do your thinking on the boat ride over.”

“Yeah, yeah,” Art sighed, getting the bottle back out of his pocket as he stood to face the door, closing their sentimental parting...

Within a few strides, he was just reaching for the doorknob when the door came open on its own. Art watched as the sharp form of Hamilton Blackforest appeared, letting himself in without so much as a second thought, stopping in mid-step when he realized he was about to collide with Art in the doorway. While he still stood there surprised, Art greeted him, “Nice knowing ya,” and stepped by to let himself out. Blackforest watched him pass with a quizzical look. After the door shut, however, he mustered himself and refocused on Horus.

“Come right in, Hamilton,” Horus jabbed, taking the appearance of the District Attorney in stride. “It’s a shame we didn’t know to expect you; we would have set a place at the table."

Blackforest folded his arms. “That’s rich, coming from you. I’m not the only one making unexpected house calls... am I, Horus?”

Horus’ brow furrowed. “You seem to have me at some disadvantage, my friend.”

“Oh don’t be coy,” Blackforest barked. “You’re doing it again, Horus. You’re doing what you always do.”

“What is that?”

“You’re taking what ought to be an open-and-shut case and making trouble.”

Horus scratched under his chin, mulling over Blackforest’s meandering accusations. “I suppose you know about my visit to the Inquisition outpost.”

"Darn straight I do," Blackforest answered sternly, seating himself at the table. His manner softened somewhat, however, as he held Horus' gaze. "Horus, did it ever cross your mind how absolutely furious the Czarina would be if she learned that you tried to go over her head like that?"

Horus sat back down across from the DA, having finished stuffing the leftover meat into a drawer. "I admit the Czarina's interest in this case does concern me, Hamilton. It was her prerogative to take the matter into the sphere of civil justice – and I'd say she did well to do so. But her involvement should have ended there. Now is the time for me to do my job, and you to do yours... the same as every other case."

Blackforest shook his head gravely. "But this isn't just like every other case. I know you'd like it to be. I understand why. But you can't impose your ideals on the reality here."

"What you really mean is, I need to align my ideals with the Czarina's."

Blackforest cocked his head, nodding. "That's another way of putting it. You know well enough that she doesn't care about the guilt or innocence of your client. This trial is about national pride. The *Czarina's* pride."

"That's not how justice works, Hamilton," Horus said, drawing himself up by his scruples. "We must judge each individual by his own conduct... not that of his nation or his race." He gave a resigned sigh. "As for the Czarina's expectations... perhaps she'd like you to convict all Mantid-kind for her. But I can only try to protect my client."

Hamilton got back up in a grumbly, subdued sort of way, adjusting his suit jacket. "I don't envy your position, Horus. I really don't. I hope somehow you can emerge from this feeling you've served that enormous conscience of yours." A fire flashed back into Blackforest's eyes. "But don't get too many more bright ideas."

Horus gave a wry grin, feeling the best he had about his prospects of mounting a meaningful defense. Nothing was quite so encouraging, after all, as Hamilton's frustration. "No promises."

Chapter 8

The impenetrable fog made Mallard shudder again, his fur bristling. The morning on the seascape was not actually all that cold... but in the face of the endless mists – a silent grey desolation hemming him in on all sides – he would never have known it. The last few days of sailing had been unnerving in their own right. Shortly after leaving Horus and Deborah, Mallard managed to attach himself to a small merchant flotilla headed for Maenea. That there were still trade ships venturing that way seemed a hopeful sign... initially. But it didn't take long before the private eye gleaned more than he wanted to from the general state of morale onboard. Apprehension hung thick over the simple cargo-laden vessel long before any fog rolled in to exasperate things. He could *smell* it, of course... fear had its own scent, if your snout was properly attuned. But beside his nose, a private eye's best tool was his ears. He'd incidentally catch snippets of conversation between crewmen, expressing doubt they'd get a chance to unload their goods. They spoke often amongst themselves of the possibility of being redirected by the Jast-Madiiran navy...

But Mallard's keen ears heard well enough what they *weren't* saying – what they refused to say. The notion of such an intervention was really just the optimistic narrative they felt comfortable sharing with each other – their unsure expressions and stunted sentences revealed as much. Behind that façade, there were other extrapolations of their future being silently contemplated... like living just long enough to be plundered by Maenean boarding parties... or perhaps having their virtually defenseless trade fleet simply sunk on sight. The farther they sailed from friendly waters, the more grim their imaginations seemed to become, until they finally reached the point where hardly anyone was speaking at all. Having no lines to read between only served to underscore the real message Art was picking up on – the message of brooding. Toxic brooding.

Now, with the culminating arrival of the dense mists, the crew appeared ready to graduate from brooding to panic. They looked hauntedly out into the nothingness, much as Art himself had surely been doing, regarding it with warring gratitude and horror. Gratitude for the providential way the fog was currently masking their final approach to Maenea. Horror at the thought of what else was hiding in there with them. Gratitude for the apparent possibility they could get in and out unnoticed. But finally horror in knowing that to complete their delivery, they would have to be discovered regardless...

Yup, Art thought to himself. *We're all gonna die*.

Steeled by this conclusion, Art spit an apricot pit over the balustrade and began a walk toward the bow. A silent pitch caught his rather poor sea-legs at unawares, and he nearly tripped over a young lady hard at work polishing some belaying hooks to an impressive shimmer. He excused himself rather absently and continued on, hopeful to find the captain and see if he could coax a candid word or two out of him...

On his way around the central hold, Mallard registered an odd snapping sound. At first, he had mistaken it for the air in the sails above him... but slowly it occurred that the sound was far too crisp. He looked up... and as he searched, he made out the source, dancing through the mists – a host of rectangular spectres. After a moment of stunned study, he realized it was a great big bunch of papers, carried along on a gentle breeze coming out of the west. Even reasoning that much, Art was quite befuddled. In his various travels, he'd seen a dandy sea-storm or two... but he'd never seen it rain *papers*...

He whipped a hand free of his pocket and snatched one of the sheets from the air as it passed low over his head. Holding it out for examination, the facing side was stamped and dated, but otherwise blank. He flipped it over...

"You're invited," he read. "Senate garden party. Kinthill Manor, 7419 Ather Ave... Yorlar, Roemnar 21210. Two weeks from printed date of circulation."

Squinting, he checked both sides of the sheet one more time before folding it and stuffing it in his pocket... still perplexed, but with nothing more to go on. Maybe the captain would know something about this strange barrage of wind-swept invitations? It was one more thing to question him about...

Sure enough, Art found him at the very nose of the ship. Captain Benthus Traligard of the *Cosigner* was easy to spot among his crew, and not just because of his enormous captainly hat – wide-brimmed but also stacked unnecessarily high with plumage. He also wore plate armor over his arms and legs – more extensive and better-fitted than regulars in the actual military. Art hadn't hesitated questioning the captain about this odd feature at their first meeting. Traligard had explained that he was always very careful to protect his extremities. Any significant amputation, after all, would mean automatic and immediate transfer to privateer work – a change in careers he meant to avoid at all costs. It seemed that Traligard's many years as a merchant had soured him on plundering. He had no wish for further participation in piracy… even if it was as part of the winning side…

"Hey there, Skipper," Art called weakly, his quiet words seeming loud indeed in that uneasy silence. To his credit, Traligard maintained his composure well, hardly even jumping before he turned.

"Good morrow, Mr. Mallard," the captain answered in hushed tones, drawing a superstitious pi symbol in the air before himself in a fast action that was obviously well-practiced. "Some spot of weather we're avin', eh?"

"That's one of the things I meant to ask about," Art replied, taking the folded paper back out of his jacket. "Does it customarily rain flyers in your neck of the woods?"

Traligard chuckled, seeming a little relieved at a quandary he could manage. "Y'd be surprised, sir, but it does. Lately, at any rate."

Art gave the flyer another look. "I can't imagine this was meant for us. Says 'Yorlar' on the address. That's a Roemnari burg, isn't it?"

"Tis, Mr. Mallard! That it surely is. I've made a delivery or two to Yorlar in my day, if y'll believe it."

Art shrugged. "I suppose even isolationists trade once in a while. If I didn't have the paper in my own hand, I'd honestly find your story much easier to believe than that I should be invited to a Heron garden party."

Traligard shook his head. "Nay, but it's just as y'said. The flyers weren't meant for the likes of us. But this ain't the first time we got a load of Roemnari mail dropped on us by accident. When the wind's in the west, it can carry their flyers for miles over open sea."

"But… why? That is, what is their mail doing floating in the air?"

There was a whimsical glint in the captain's eye just then, as is customary any time a sailor is given an opportunity to spin a yarn. "I've heard tell the Postmaster General of the Archipelago is something of an innovator. Story is he leveraged a small fleet of mothballed Bombers from the Roemnari Air Force, and he's been experimenting with them as means of deliverin' anything meant for broad, indiscriminate circulation. Royal decrees, public announcements, Dronehood surveys, various types of junk mail. Only they ain't so precise with their payloads yet. A lot of it ends up out here with us, in the drink."

"Huh," Art replied. "And Roemnar's usually so good at keeping a tight lid on their business." He held the flyer out. "I'll bet if we all showed up at the garden party with one of these, they'd teach their mailmen to fly lower in a hurry."

Captain Traligard laughed. "Aye, no doubt they would."

The moment of levity was welcome to both men as they stood there in the haze, but it quickly vanished, their collective attention drawn back into the wispy uncertainty before them.

"Nervous, Cap?" Art asked.

"This isn't my first trade war, Mr. Mallard," Traligard remarked as he scanned, "not by a long fathom. I think I know by now when the other countries of the Archipelago are just groaning about high prices, and when they're really ready to start shooting."

Art nodded as more hope slipped out of him. The captain was no more confident than anybody. A well-rehearsed line like that confirmed it. "Uh-huh."

Traligard spun to confront his bit of derision. "Not convinced, sir? Well, maybe it will ease your mind to know – there are goods in these holds, the likes of which you can be sure the Maeneans would pay dearly for right now."

"Oh yeah? What kind of goods?"

"Cannonballs."

Art had to admit, that was somewhat more encouraging – if only in a fleeting and ironic sort of way.

They watched quietly for some time after that, with no sign of the passage of time. The fog remained stifling – the world, apparently unmoving. Art's sense of watchful claustrophobia was getting to him. Every little ruffle in the sails or lap of wave against the bow was like a traitor's horn, sounding their position for the enemy. Finally, Captain Traligard leaned over the bow…

"See something, skipper?" Art asked.

No immediate answer.

"Nay," Traligard hushed at last. "But they're close. I can feel it in my plate armor."

Hardly a moment later, his feelings proved true. Dark silhouettes of tall ships began to draw up before them like ghouls. The smaller merchant fleet made silent course adjustments. In the shadow of the Maenean blockade, it was all they could do to set course around the warships, and wait breathlessly to see whether they would be allowed past the long rows of cannons... or *not*...

Mallard, for his part, recalled knowing well enough the backwater proclivities of the country of Maenea. They fought older kinds of wars, with older kinds of weapons. Their ships were certainly not the sleek fashion-plates of modern warfare that his own Jast-Madiir employed. Yes, he could remind himself of these facts all he wanted. But here, in *their* waters, under *their* guns, it offered no assurance. He was better off simply reminding himself to breathe.

Breathe he did – once in a great while – as time and silence magnified one another. Tension mounted, daring any sudden calamity at all to come along and snap it. Finally, Art was jolted by a sudden crash! All eyes spun to the source, only to see a clumsy crewman had simply toppled a mop bucket... his teeth clenched in a grin of horrified humiliation. The collective sigh of the crew might have blown away the fog...

As the Cosigner at last pulled astride the Maenean galleons, it finally seemed clear that there would be no shooting. Maeneans were a bit of an odd bunch at times, perhaps, but they were bright enough not to catch each other in a crossfire. While the air cleared of all present doubt, Art realized for the first time that he had a death-grip on the baluster. He had a time of it, getting his claws unstuck as he relaxed.

"And people wonder why I turned an early grey," he remarked to himself none too quietly.

"That was a bit touch-and-go, it seemed," the captain agreed. "But we ought to be clear from now on."

"Still, I'll feel a lot better once we make port. How long do you make that, Cap? Any estimates?"

Traligard shook his head, a rather puzzled look on his face. "I'm afraid y've got it wrong, sir. Nay, we don't make port on the *Cosigner*." He checked around them slyly, and leaned in for sake of discretion. "Half my crew is high flight risk, y'see."

"Shanghaied?" Art asked.

"Aye. So we unload our wares on other trade ships. I'm afraid y'll have to be deboarding to a Maenean craft, not Maenea itself."

Art sighed. "Wish I'd known that upfront. What am I supposed to do to cross over? Are you going to list me as part of the cargo manifest?"

"I would, except I ain't no privateer, so I can't sell y'off." He shrugged. "Not sure Maeneans are in the shanghai business anyway."

"What does that leave then?"

Traligard shook his head. "I'm afraid I've no idea, Mr. Mallard. Nothing like this has come up before, in all m'years. But I wish ya best of luck, thinkin' of something. That I do."

Art huffed. "Yeah. I've been getting that a lot lately."

* * *

Perhaps an hour later, the *Cosigner* had cast lines to a Maenean counterpart, and the two ships were bustling with moving merchandise. Art finally resolved on a simple plan. He grabbed a crate, hauled it over to the Maenean ship, and then, when he was sure no one was looking, he got his invite flyer back out, unfolded it, and held it up in front of his face. The little sheet was a far cry from the newspaper he was accustomed to wielding to attain total anonymity, but being in a pinch, he strained himself to make do. And it proved enough. While he sat on the deck, eyes buried in the little paper, no Maenean merchant-marine troubled him. He grew rather cramped, and severely bored, focusing on the sparse information for hours while he waited for the ship to make port. But at last, they reached land, and in a last flourish of stealth he walked down the gangplank with his flyer and quickly slipped away...

* * *

Once away from the docks, Art didn't find any further need to disguise his comings and goings. A random private investigator might be suspect on a ship he had not arranged to be on... but in the countryside, no one would question it. Thus, he wandered freely about the Maenean town – a busy place, if more than a little rustic next to his homeland. Asking around, he quickly learned that he was in Port Mauraisa, very near Maenea's secondary isle of Magna Koepna – much further north and east than he would have expected, but still fortuitously close to some of the country's Mantid-infested jungles. Inquiring about the linguist Jojojo, however, he had somewhat less success. His first real lead was a guy that set him on the trail of a local xenobiologist named Grover – somebody that the Meduseldan had been known to trade notes with in the past. When asked for Grover's address, the guy had said, "The tavern's down the street."

Standing outside the modest establishment – quaintly named 'Definitely Food Restaurant and Tavern' – Art took a moment to scratch his chin thoughtfully. He wasn't sure why every mundane little escapade always seemed to involve a trip into a questionable watering hole, but such was life. As he shrugged it off and reached for the double door, however, a tall and scraggly man with a haunting stare burst out just in front of him. For a moment, they just stood in place, each looking quite startled at the other...

"Don't go in there, Boyo," the man said, his voice as scraggly as his bristly face. "There's a wild-eyed hill-man in there who'll corner ya with his political nonconformity, *soon as look at ya*!!"

Art examined the man, unsure – trying to imagine finding someone in the tavern who was more wild-eyed than he was. "I'm afraid I have no choice, friend," Art replied at last, politely as he was able. "I'm looking for a xenobiologist named Grover."

The man grabbed him by the shoulders, somehow managing to look even more stunned. "Yer lookin' for *me*?"

Art blinked. "Apparently."

After a moment of setting his jaw, the man Grover searched past Art's huge shoulders in a flurry of action. "Well, alright, let's go somewhere." Without further ado, he started to walk away.

"Okay. Like where?" Art called after.

"Anyplace but here, Boyo."

* * *

Grover threw down his fifth flagon of grape juice, wiping his mouth with a red-stained sleeve. Seeing that his immediate supply was exhausted, he took his first notice of Art Mallard since sitting down. "It's a hard life for a scientist in this country, Boyo."

"Any harder, and you'd need gills," Art agreed.

Grover turned his glass around thoughtfully. "There was a time when I was respectable, ya know. Admired. Used to clean stables for a livin'. An honorable profession, that." He shook his head. "Lots and lots of honor in that line of work."

"Among other things," Mallard quipped.

Grover turned his eyes on Art, pointing at him. "And heritage! Ya wanna talk about a sturdy, dependable, traditional job? *Ha*! Cleanin' stables ain't changed once since the invention of the shovel."

"A fortuitous invention, I would think."

Grover huffed. "One of the few, Boyo. One of the very few." He sighed. "Science ain't done the world many favors. We don't take to it, here in Maenea. Tried and true – that be our way. Only thing is... science makes money. Thus it beguiled our fair Countess. What with the Great Horse Shortage and all, I was one of the unlucky few ta be drafted into her new industry of research. Now me wife and children won't even speak ta me. 'Fraid I'll fill their heads with all manner of new-fangled notions."

Art winced. "Isn't xenobiology just the study of different sentient life forms?"

Grover shook his cupped hands in a gesture of bewildered incredulity. "That's what I been tryin' to tell me kin from day one, Boyo! The Countess – bless her stewardly self – ain't no fanatic. She courted science with caution. Purely observational fields. I ain't out ta invent nothin'... just jot down some notes about things that been around for thousands o' years. Ain't no harm in that... is there?" His eyes were pleading.

Art shrugged. "Probably not."

The xenobiologist's shoulders slumped as he breathed his relief. Art's nose twitched in mild disgust.

"Many thanks to ya, Boyo. I needed ta hear that. It's been hard ta cope lately. Me family's disowned me, the journal's breathin' down me neck, and the cup goes dry too soon." As if catching himself, Grover suddenly went wide-eyed again, and pale. "And speakin' of the journal... what was it ya wanted to see me about?" he asked cautiously. "I'll have somethin' ta write up soon, I promise. I just need a week or a month or two more and that's all... and I mean it this time..."

"Relax, Mac," Art replied. "I'm not here to collect on your work. I'm not actually here about you at all. I'm trying to get in touch with a linguist. One by the name of... Jojojo?"

Grover just stared at him blankly for a tense moment, until at last he sat back, chuckling low and ominous. "That's not how he pronounces it."

Art's ears perked. "So you do know him."

"I do, but that's the long and short of it. If ya came ta me hoping ta find him, yer outta luck, Boyo. 'Bout the only thing I can do for ya is offer a chair, and we can both sit here and wait him out t'gether."

Art searched him unflinching, determined to be sure he'd got a straight answer. "You don't have any way of reaching him at all?"

Grover laughed more openly, if not less ominously. "On me life, I don't! If I did, I'd be a sight less desperate right now. That supercilious old Taltax has all the field notes I need ta publish the research paper I owe the state. That is, if he remembered to take any such notes..."

Art's head went askance. "You have the linguist taking your field notes for you?"

He folded his arms. "I do. And I think ya'd be inclined ta do likewise, in my place, rather than wander out among the Mantid tribes and collect them yerself. They're the species I promised ta study. Seemed like a cinch, back when I was cuttin' a deal with the linguist. Nowhere in the observational sciences rulebook did it say I had ta publish me own observations. Only I ne'er thought he'd stay in the jungle so long..."

"Why not?"

"I didn't call him a supercilious old Taltax for nothin'. He's got a big head alright... or he would, if he had any head a'tall. But more than that, he's *old*. A *real* old timer. Like, maybe got a year or two left. Then *poof*! He'll be gone."

Art took a moment to let that roll around in his head. It was a firmly established fact of nature that Meduseldan drones poofed out of existence at the very moment they attained the age of 140 years. Thoughtfully, he took that air-dropped garden party invitation back out of his pocket... careful not to look at it too intently, lest Grover wonder where he'd gone. An idea was forming in his mind... a desperate gambit. There may yet be a way to reach out to Jojojo, he decided. A way that, fortunately, wasn't quite so desperate as charging into the woods in person...

"What is it, Boyo?" Grover put in. "What are ya hatchin' behind that smart snout o' yers?"

Art was a bit surprised that his musing had been so overt... perhaps he had been longer in thought than he reckoned. But he didn't look up from his invite right off. "I'm thinking the answer to both our problems is blowing in the wind, friend," he replied at length. Finally, he gave Grover another searching look. "Tell me, Grover... do you by chance have any favors you can call in with the Postmaster General?"

Grover nodded, putting his lip out rather smugly. "Wouldn't be much of a xenobiologist if I didn't."

Chapter 9

Horus sat sternly in the folding seat by the glass, staring straight into the eye-clusters of his client, trying his best to project an aura of man-to-man solemnity. Since Art left, he'd made visits like this every day. Unlike their first meeting, there had been no more throwing of meat... and certainly no more shots fired. Rather than insult the bug by trying to bribe back his confidence, Horus meant to level with him, if he could. But a bug-face proved a hard thing to read. For the Mantid's part, he probably found Horus' face every bit as inscrutable...

"What's going on in that head of yours?" he wondered aloud, his client utterly motionless, not so much as flinching at the sudden sound of his voice. "Are you still just waiting to see what horrible thing I do next?" He shook his head subtly. "How could you guess I'm the only friend you have here?"

The bug's mandibles oscillated.

Horus grinned.

"You'll know it before all this is over. Even if Art never finds that linguist, I'll find a way to let you know. Every one of us needs an advocate. You should understand you have one."

No further fidgeting came from his client. No sign – nothing to interpret. Horus nodded, if only to himself. That was alright. There was a lot of time left... *time*, and little else to fill it with...

Today, however, would be somewhat different. Today Horus had more than one reason to be here. There was a final thread of investigation for him to snatch up, and see where it led him...

At once, the heavy door squealed open behind Horus. As he turned, the dogged but energetic form of Captain Alexei sped in. "Top of the morning, Counselor," he called out as he crossed the room on his stilted legs.

"Good morning..." Horus began, folding his ears back as he got a better look, "...Captain?" He couldn't help being a little taken back, seeing that, while the cuts all over Alexei's face had improved, his left eye was all but invisible this morning – buried, in effect, under a serious shiner. Horus watched as the exuberance on the Captain's face disappeared, his brow knitting with concern...

"What is it, Mr. Templar? You look rather like you've seen a ghost."

"I'm getting to where I expect to, the next time I see you," Horus admitted.

After a moment of confusion, Alexei snapped with recognition. "It's the eye, isn't it?" he asked expectantly.

Horus didn't even bother to nod. "You look like you tried to stop a speeding pachycephalosaurus. What on earth happened this time?"

"Nothing strictly new; just more fallout from the cat incident. The Fire Chief took it rather hard, when he found out I impinged on his jurisdiction." As he spoke, Alexei's high spirits began to deflate, his visible eye meandering into some sullen distance.

"I'm sorry you've had such a rough week," Horus cheered him.

Alexei chuckled. "Is it so obvious? Yes, I suppose it has been a rough week."

"The way you've been mauled and mangled? I should say so."

He shook his head. "It's not that. By all accounts, it should have been a *good* week. I could not have hoped for a more fortuitous string of misfortunes! The real trouble is... the Deputy Constable has yet to seem even the least impressed with my hardihood. If anything, I could swear he becomes *more* skeptical of me with every injury I incur! The man is a very tough egg to crack. I begin to worry that I am, indeed, not hardscrabble enough to be a city cop, after all. And beside all that, the bill to have my glasses replaced will be exorbitant!"

Horus might have explained Miloje's irritation right then and there, but something unaccountable made him hesitate. From his vantage, it was plain that Alexei was going to great pains to prove a moot point, and only making a sideshow of himself in the eyes of the Deputy Constable in the process. *Why don't I just* tell *him that*? he mused, careening through his own headspace. Did he not have the heart to quash the young man's ingenuous worldview? No, it wasn't just that. But whatever more there was... he couldn't yet determine. Still, by now Horus trusted his lawyerly instincts. He'd go along with Alexei's delusions, for now... with the private resolution of making things right later. Though as he considered Alexei's many present disfigurements, he knew he'd better not make it *too* much later...

With the lull in conversation, the Captain snatched down his own bobby, tumbling it as he apologetically switched topics. "Anyway, there is the business at hand. Regrettably, I was sent ahead to ask you to leave, Mr. Templar. Your client's regular visiting hours are going to have to be disrupted by other business today."

Horus grinned a crooked grin. "I am aware. And I thank you for your polite invitation to leave. I'm afraid I must politely decline."

Alexei looked up from his hat with a bit of shock, but had no chance to respond before the sound of the door intruded again. The Deputy Constable himself had arrived, along with a whole ensemble of sturdy policemen.

"Ah, Templar – fancy meeting you here," Miloje projected, crossing the room at a much slower clip. "I've come to collect your client for an appointment of a different sort. But I expect the Captain was just informing you of this and seeing you out." Miloje gave Alexei a bit of a look.

"Good morning, Milo," Horus greeted him. "You may rest assured I am well aware of my client's other appointment – that is, his checkup with Dr. Nokkaeru. Your good Captain here has advised me to leave with all due discretion and courtesy. Even so, I'll have to insist on staying, regardless of his urgings... or yours."

Miloje huffed, a bit of a twinkle in his eye. If there was one thing the Deputy Constable seemed to enjoy, it was a bout of well-mannered verbal jousting.

"Wandering into overlapping spheres of confidentiality, aren't we? Surely a defense lawyer can appreciate the sacred trust between doctor and patient."

"Not so sacred that the SAPD has seen fit to go without full knowledge of his medical records... all of which were generated right here in this building."

Miloje shrugged. "You wouldn't seriously expect us to send him to the hospital, would you? It's not our fault he was interned here first. Anyway, we procured the proper permissions for those records."

Horus produced a rolled-up sheet of paper. "So have I." He held out a subpoena addressed to Dr. Nokkaeru for Miloje to see. Miloje reached for it...

"I can serve that for you, if you like, Counselor. No need to inconvenience yourself..."

"Ah, but I insist," Horus said, retracting the paper. It was a bit of a ruse – the Doctor was already prominent on Blackforest's list of witnesses, and so didn't strictly need to be served papers by him. But Horus was willing to take a chance Miloje didn't know that, or wouldn't call him on it... if it meant he could confer with her in the process of her work. "You're a busy man, Milo... and I, an underworked Public Defender, with nothing but time on his hands."

The self-satisfied look in Miloje's eye only brightened, even as he seemed to lose the joust. "Suit yourself, Templar," he waved dismissively, turning to go. "But at least one of us ought to have the good sense to avoid that witchdoctor, wherever possible. Stay if you wish. I'm leaving." The Deputy Constable always managed a parting jab.

* * *

Truth be told, Horus shared Miloje's sentiments. He would have preferred to avoid meeting the SAPD's resident plague doctor... perhaps more so even than Miloje himself, even if he was decidedly less vocal about it. Watching the team of policemen bind his client to the operating table, Horus empathized, feeling similarly constrained by his sworn duty. Both of them were unflinching in the face of the unwanted company coming to call. But both of them would have willed themselves to disappear, if they could have...

Of course, drawing such comparisons was a bit of a conceit. Dr. Nokkaeru had never dissected, reconstructed, sewn, stitched, or so much as prodded Horus. In their few meetings, she didn't even treat him with the cold, standoffish disinterest that made everyone else around her feel like little more in her eyes than dead toads to be practiced on. No, it was worse than that. She was *nice* to him. 'Well hello, Counselor Templar'... 'So good to see you again, Counselor Templar.' Always something like that. Coming from such a macabre personality, congeniality felt like a curse. Worst of all, Horus had not the slightest idea what had ever inspired her to single him out this way...

"Ah! Well-met, Counselor Templar," Dr. Nokkaeru's voice eschewed from the doorway, the very moment she passed into the room. Horus' fur crawled. "So good of you to grace us with your presence this morning." He searched her inflections, hopeful to find some hint of sarcasm. There was none. "Do tell me... how have you been?" Her tone was anticipant....

"I've been well, thank you," Horus replied with practiced cordiality.

"...Oh..." the Doctor replied, suddenly quite crestfallen. Her reaction cracked Horus' diplomatic front – he blinked quizzically...

"...How have *you* been?"

She waved a dismissive talon before continuing past him to the operating table. "That is both irrelevant and inconclusive. Let us instead determine the welfare of your client. His wound has thus far healed well, if that will comfort you."

"It is primarily about the wound that I meant to speak with you," Horus said, steeling himself now against the possibility of getting an answer he didn't want. "What do you suppose was the cause of it?" He gulped ever so discretely as he came to the real crux of the matter. "Any chance it was some steel-forged weapon or other?"

"No indeed, Counselor," she answered. Horus was greatly relieved. Physical evidence connecting his client to any kind of brush with Jast-Madiir regulars would have been all Hamilton needed to shut the case before it could even be properly opened. But as she unwrapped the bandaging, she continued... "The trauma is consistent with damage from a raptorial foreleg, such as the creature itself possesses... though his assailant would have been approximately 30 or 40 percent larger than he."

This unsolicited bit of information hit Horus like a sack full of bricks... but not at all in a bad way. Rather, he felt distinctly that these were the bricks of providence. His client had evidently been attacked by another Mantid... a *much bigger* Mantid. "30 to 40 percent, you say? How do you account for that?" A hopeful thought occurred to him. "Is my client not yet fully grown? An adolescent... or even a *child*?" Even the Czarina would be sure to lose some of her bloodlust, if she learned the Mantid was a minor. At the very least, she'd likely commute his execution until he was older...

"No," Dr. Nokkaeru replied. "This is assuredly an adult male of average size and build." Horus mentally snapped his fingers at the abrupt loss of a brief, beautiful hope. Still, her answer only invited more questions...

"That's somewhat baffling. That is, I had thought he was a bit on the *small* side. To learn that creatures of such limited stature have been Jast-Madiir's only unassailable adversaries is, well..." he paused mid-sentence as his train of thought returned to the overriding question, "...and what about this mysterious, exceptionally large Mantid that attacked him?"

"It is all quite simple," she explained. "Inter-Tribal warfare is a mainstay of the Mantid social construct. But their warrior caste is not comprised of males. It is the *female* of their species that is the larger and stronger specimen. One may easily infer that this average male's village fell victim to an average sort of attack... and he, to injury by an average female's foreleg. Indeed, it is highly unlikely that there is anything exceptional about his story at all... aside from his grave misfortune in having been discovered by your countrymen."

This proved a lot to digest in short order for Horus. He had meant to learn all he could about the bug's injury from the Doctor… and to glean what he may from any uncommon knowledge a Roemnari might possess about Mantids in general… but this trove of information far exceeded his wildest expectations…

"Well how do you like that?" he chuckled, shaking his head in wonder. "So much for the Czarina's hardened enemy of the state. He really *is* no fighter after all."

"I had to wonder about his being charged with war crimes," Nokkaeru admitted. "But I should have known all along it was done in ignorance. The entire tribunal to come will be no better than a farce."

Horus reached back into his inner pocket and produced the subpoena. "I'd be much-obliged if you would express that opinion again in open court."

As he reached out to hand it to her, she accepted the document. "I will… for what little it may avail you, Counselor. I doubt very much if any arguments or appeals to reason will turn aside the wrath of your state. Malicious intent… guilt by association… inasmuch as District Attorney Blackforest can keep the jury focused on the Mantid's agency alone, his conviction remains inevitable, in my estimation of your legal system."

Horus frowned. "That would be my estimation as well. Still, at least there's some hope now. If only Art can make it back with that Meduseldan linguist, perhaps I'll learn something more that I can use."

The Doctor's leather fittings crinkled as she returned to her work. "Yet if my testimony does not sway them, any from your client on his own behalf certainly won't."

Horus couldn't help being a little frustrated by her insistence – intentional or otherwise – on batting him back and forth between being hopeful and demoralized. He folded his arms. "Would you mind telling me what I ought to try instead?"

She got some manner of unnecessarily gruesome looking scraper out of her medical case. "You are endeavoring to *tell* the jurors that this Mantid is no monster. You must *show* them, if you can." She went to scrape the bug's exposed wound. "A stubborn mind may dismiss even the best carefully-worded argument. You must concentrate on the universal… the undeniable." The Mantid thrashed against its bindings as she began collecting flakes of his scab. The Doctor abruptly shouted in his face, "*Be still, creature, or I will give you a matching one on the other side!!!*" He clammed up tight as a drum. She turned her spectral mask on Horus. "There, you see?

He understands... though my speech means nothing to his mind. There are truths and intentions too plain for words."

Horus himself felt somewhat petrified. "I'll keep that in mind," he said, brow furrowing.

"But enough about your case," Dr. Nokkaeru said, just as Horus was about to pick up a foot and begin his escape. "Let us discuss *you*."

"...Me?" Horus objected, rather dumbfounded. "We've already exchanged formalities... talked business. Pardon my asking, but... what more could you want? My life story?"

"Some portion of it or other, yes," she answered evenly, placing her scraping instrument in a graduated cylinder of clear liquid... watching as it turned blue... nodding. "But whether it is a part of your story which has already been, or has yet to be, I cannot say." She shot him another piercing look. "Is there any great tragedy in your past, Counselor?"

Horus really was beside himself with this one. He'd known some characters in his line of work, but he tended to be the one asking intrusive questions, rather than the other way around. Even so, perhaps despite himself, he wound up forming an answer...

"I've had some... unfortunate drama in the family, yes. But I don't see..."

"...Oh, nothing so mundane as that," she interjected. "The deaths and disagreements of close relations are just white noise... a suffering common to all. I am talking about something on a grander scale. A true *calamity*. Have you ever had one of those?"

If Horus' face soured somewhat, even *he* could hardly help it. "No."

"Hmm..." the Doctor mused at length. "That is unfortunate. You'll have to excuse my being so forthright... it seems I shall have to wait for my answers regardless."

Horus – all but wroth from her wearying eccentricities – stood in waning expectation of her to explain herself. "Wait?" he finally asked. "You mean, wait for some... *calamity*... to befall me?"

She nodded. "Yes."

At last, it dawned on him... he was talking to a Heron. Dire Herons were known to have peculiar powers of insight. In particular – though it was quite rare – some were even precognitive... able to glimpse the future...

"You..." he stammered, "...you have the gift... the ability to see through time?"

"*See*? Hardly," she answered, nearly laughing as she began rebandaging the Mantid. "Yet even those without sight may fumble about in the dark. I *feel* a tragedy about you, Counselor Templar… one of sublime quality, which I have felt in few others. So you see, I could hardly help but be curious."

He shook his head. "More than idly curious. It honestly sounds like you'd enjoy collecting some tale of my misfortune."

"Mine is the business of misfortune," she explained. "If I've learned to appreciate its finer attributes, that is no worse than pragmatism on my part. It was, upon a time, an Imperial virtue to find joy in misery, though few of us ever truly mastered it. If we had, perhaps we would still be governing the foolish fates of the world."

"Well, in that case, I commend you for your high scruples… and I thank you for giving me so much to look forward to." He politely inclined himself, then made a belabored pivot toward the door. "I think I'll be going now."

"There is no need," she said, snipping off the roll of gauze. "I am finished here. You may remain with your client, if you wish." She closed the lid on her case. "He is quite healthy."

Horus was aware that his features betrayed some immediate relief. He hoped she would attribute it to the good health of his client, and not her sudden departure. But even as she was leaving the room and might have left him to a dubious reprieve, he had a sudden thought…

"Oh, Doctor!" he called.

She stopped, stepping foot back in the room. "Yes, Counselor?"

"Since you've expressed some skill at gauging people's misfortunes, I wonder… how would you rate my client?"

She trained her goggles on the bug. After a moment or two of studious consideration, she made her assessment. "He would seem to fare no better than the everyman." With that, she was nearly gone again… until, this time, she stopped herself. "But then, I do not sense he will fare much *worse*, either."

With that final contemplative remark, she departed. Horus sighed and relaxed… and not just from her absence. He hoped against reason his client could read the affirmation in his face. After all, the everyman's ills didn't tend to include being put to death in an alien land. Maybe there was cause for optimism yet…

Chapter 10

Art felt more than a little dumb sitting on the hillside with his hands in his pockets. A light drizzle had just rolled in, adding to his dumb feelings. He thought about his entire ensemble of really nifty umbrellas on a nice mahogany rack in an undisclosed location back in Jast-Madiir. Why a bright guy like him had neglected to bring even one of them along on an international caper presently eluded him. One way or another, he was out in the elements with no remedy. At Grover's insistence, they'd left Port Mauraisa far behind and below, having chosen the rolling, grassy summit of Finnigan's Tumble as their rendezvous point. A hill too modest and benign to be a 'Peak' or 'Leap', 'Tumble' was the most thrilling label anyone could have hoped to attach to it... and even that appeared to be a stretch. If this 'Finnigan' had tumbled more than a few feet, he must've been one clumsy oaf.

Art wasn't sure why he was letting the dull, unthreatening nature of the hill get to him. But as he slowly progressed from feeling soggy to downright soaked, so he grew surlier. His ears were getting tired from pinning themselves back against the flanks of his very suave investigator hat. His fingers were still blistered and cramped from days of writing the same few dratted lines over and over and over again. And still he had to sit there cold and wet, looking stupidly into the sky. It wasn't within the wheelhouse of Mesomelae to growl, exactly, but he had certainly reached the point of wanting to grumble to himself...

"What are we doing out here in the middle of nowhere, anyway?" he asked, the question finally boiling out of him. "Couldn't we have just as well stayed in town? Maybe standing in a nice warm post office?"

"Not hardly," Grover replied. "The middle of nowhere is just where we need to be, Boyo. Or 'tany rate, it's where I need to be. Me reputation is already in shambles, what with bein' a scientist now, and all. I sure don't need ta be seen in the company of the Postmaster General, when he comes thunderin' in. That'd be all it would take ta cement me legacy as a pariah, for good and for sure."

"Well, he's more than welcome to come 'thundering in' any time now," Art quipped, taking out his swank pocket watch.

"He won't be late, if that's yer mind. You needn't worry 'bout that. Not by rain, snow, sleet, hail, slime landslides, regular landslides, tornados, hurricanes, tornados inside of hurricanes, cosmic collisions or smudged forwarding addresses will the post e'er be deterred."

Art huffed. "And how about light drizzles? I don't know what time you're on Grover, but my watch says he's got a minute and 23 seconds. Then he'll be late. You realize this isn't an actual mail carrier we're dealing with here. This is a big-wig – a high-roller – the coolest cat in the postal world... at least here in the Archipelago. And we simply sent him a letter asking him to be here by noon today. I've got a nickel that says he doesn't even show."

Grover knelt next to where Art sat on the ground, looking stern and steely into his soul. "Mind yer words, Boyo. General Rutherford Cortez D'Allemagne *is* the Post of Idriulthoronta – and he sure as shoot didn't get that way by accident. That facetted little head o' his be like a prism, through which the radiance of their paragon Klaiven forever shines. He could no sooner be late than you nor I could willfully burp up our own appendix."

"I don't even have an appendix," Art explained.

"My point exactly."

Art shook his head. "With a personality that dogged, I'd think you were talking about an Inquisitor."

Grover grimaced. "I can see I'll have to do all the talkin'. For an investigator, yer pretty thick on a few things. All an Inquisitor's got is *rules*... but the Post Man, now... he's got *virtues*. There's a world a'difference."

Art shrugged. "You're the expert. I haven't had many dealings with these postal types before... certainly none with the General himself. I'll be interested to meet him."

Grover nodded. "As will I."

Art's ears snapped up. "You mean... you *haven't* met him?"

"No," Grover answered indifferently. "What gave ya that idea?"

Before Art could even begin to snap back at him, a distant thrumming pulsed against his finely-tuned eardrums. A brooding and powerful noise growing quickly in potency bounded off the landscape and rattled around in his huge chest. The sound was soon so oppressive he felt like he was presently being landed on... but no matter how he searched the skies, he still could see nothing. He found himself on his feet, not remembering the act of standing – some reflex inside him must've decided that he didn't want to be caught sitting down as the sky conspired to squash him...

"------------- --- -- ----- --- - -----!" he saw Grover mouth through the gale of concussive sound, and he heartily agreed.

After a goodly interval of deafening racket, the source of the thrumming appeared – a towering flying vessel whipping dark clouds out of its way, roiling sheets of otherwise placid rain with huge propellors. The noise notwithstanding, Art was rather taken aback by it all. He was aware of the existence of such craft and understood their basic function in principle. But he'd never *experienced* one before. Jast-Madiir was a rich and posh land with many modern accoutrements, as Human lands go... but even millennia after the fall of their glorious Empire, the Dire Herons still possessed all manner of instruments that far exceeded the sophistication found in rival states. This grand vertical foil swooping down on them was a Roemnari Bomber – one of old make, and not even necessarily in the best state of upkeep, Art knew. That, after all, was the sort of vehicle he'd been told the Postmaster General had appropriated for his experiments in mass mail airdrops... and the very vehicle Grover had asked him to bring to their meeting, at Art's urging...

At last, the boom of the propellors relaxed a bit as the throttle was drawn back. Art scarcely had the time or presence of mind to wonder how the thing was supposed to finish its approach without crashing into the hill when it rather abruptly stopped and spun, slowly settling toward the ground, evidently suspended by lighter-than-air ballast. From the rear of the airship (which was now facing them), an incredibly long ramp extended, heralding a very regal figure as he strode dauntless down into their midst on his five spindly legs, fur-lined cape mesmerizing as it fluttered in the bluster.

With a labored blink, Art freed himself from a measure of the dread wonder that had befallen him and Grover – just enough that he reached once more for his pocket watch. In a grandiose flurry of convergence, his eyes caught the second hand precisely as it struck noon... the very instant the Postmaster General's frontmost leg planted itself on the Maenean turf. Their meeting had convened.

"Well, bless my triangles!" a most commanding voice called out, drowning the failing sound of the Bomber's turbines as it finally settled to the hillside, balancing airily on the end of its tall central fin. Floating out of a pocket as if on unseen hands, the General polished up a monocle with the hem of his cape before setting it in front of his capsule-head. Whether it was daylight or some of that radiant virtue Grover had spoken of, a disarming glint in that monocle searched them each in turn. "Which of you gents is the xenobiologist Grover? Which of you has called in his favor, most duly owed? Let him declare himself! Let his request be heard."

In the seconds that followed, neither man stirred. Mallard studied the General for a spell, managing to convince himself that he was more professionally curious than awed. The man was, of course, a Phage – one of a subrace of bacteriophages the Creators had enlarged to macroscopic organisms many centuries ago – nearly all men of the Post were. As such, he had a 'head' like crystal and a body like some living machine – burnished, unyielding... all simple geometry. Between his bearing, his authority, precision, and impressive display of formidable resources, the fact that he stood no higher than three feet on his insectoid legs subtracted nothing from his great stature...

As impressed as Art was, Grover was evidently feeling much further out of his depth. Art dramatically cleared his throat in the hopes of getting the whole council going again. Fortunately, the ruckus seemed to snap Grover out of his trance...

"Uh, er, yes, that's me. I'm Grover."

"Ah, capital! The proprietor of 5313 Backabbey Way Port Mauraisa, Maenea 10049! How nice to finally have a face to go with the box." He turned to face Art. "And you, sir?"

"Artimus Mallard," Artimus Mallard answered with a slight nod.

"Egad!" the General exclaimed, his monocle flipping up in the air as he recoiled. "Surely not *the* Artimus Mallard of PO Box 4249 St. Argonsburg, Jast-Madiir 41011-0934?! You are a long way from home, my good man! Did you know there is a trade war on?"

"I noticed," Art replied.

"He has journeyed far in search of another, but he found only me," Grover put in. "Now he begs this favor of you, O General."

"*He*?" the General protested. "But I understood this was *your* favor."

"This *is* his favor," Art explained. "I'm here to help you help him, which also helps me."

"I see..." General Rutherford went along, slowly nodding his polyhedral head. "That is some thread to take up. And still we've not come to the part where you explain what this favor is you want. I hope you'll take more care with that."

Art promptly spun and took a few strides further up the hill, hefting four big, heavy canvas bags. He returned and presented them before the General. "What we want is simple," he began. "We've spent the last few days making hundreds of flyers. We wanted you to bring your Bomber so that you can make a mass drop over the jungles to the south-west, here."

He nodded in the general direction of the trees. "That's really all. Although, if you're feeling quite generous, you could stick around and give us all a lift back to St. Argonsburg."

"Us *all*?" General Rutherford plied. "Are there more in this helpful conspiracy of yours?"

"If all goes to plan, there'll be a third when this is through."

"We've another man in the jungle," Grover leapt in. "But we've no other way ta get hold of him. Your Bomber is our only hope."

"Hmm..." General Rutherford mused as he began to pace, his frontmost leg tinking against his head while he tapped it thoughtfully. "The flyers shall have to be inspected. I would have preferred that you had my people make them up to your specifications... or else enlisted the help of the Clerks. But come now! Join me inside." He waved them back up his ramp.

Art felt his gut seize up with sudden doubt. He hadn't expected the flyer would be looked at. He'd hoped they would simply dump the bagfuls into some kind of ammunition tanks and proceed straight away. This was an unexpected complication...

* * *

"Welcome aboard, gentlemen," General Rutherford said as they ducked through the rear entrance of the Bomber... already too high in the air for Art's taste. "Allow me to introduce my crew: First and Second Bombardiers Madeline Vincente and Romero Lautrec..." he gestured to two Phage wearing combat helmets, "...Flight Engineer Antoine Perez..." another Phage holding a big wrench in midair, "...and Pilot Yvonne de la Mancha," a final Phage with goggles. "They are exceptional men and women of the Post, one and all. Given a few hours, we shall have all of your flyers vetted. Only let me see one now, before I commit to any further investigation."

Art grimaced, still bracing himself against what the General might think of their flyer, trying to figure how he might weasel out of this step...

"Pardon my asking, General, but isn't it against the Postal Code or something to look at people's mail?"

"Oh dear yes, quite so," the General nodded. "Though there is no 'Postal Code' as such... only the principles that quietly shimmer in all of our souls – certainly much too profound to be written into mere words – and spoken of only for the benefit of outsiders, such as yourselves. Even so, the part of the

'Code' you speak of applies to personal correspondence. Mass mail must be screened."

Darn it, Art thought, as he reluctantly reached into a bag and grabbed a flyer. "Well, okay," he said aloud, trying to be nonchalant, but sounding unsure despite himself. "Here ya go."

General Rutherford took hold of the paper as with some invisible limb. He searched it up and down for a spell as Art and Grover held their breath...

"Event flyer... sturdy bleached kraft paper... 85 white... crayon lettering – interesting choice."

"We hoped the wax would be weatherproof," Art explained. "And anyway we ran out of ink about two hundred copies in."

"Good fortune I should think..." Rutherford almost muttered, as in deep thought. "Crayon will indeed fare better." He shook his head. "But to have some in both ink and wax? That does not well adhere to any one template." Art just about bit his lip – the General already sounded disapproving, and he hadn't even got to the substance of the flyer yet... "And what of this postage *date*?!" he plied suddenly. "Maypril 35th, 9020 S.E.? That is over four years out..."

Art made a show of shrugging it off. "I understand you guys are pretty against being late."

"Indeed. 'Death before tardiness', one might say."

"Well... is it really so bad if you're a little early instead? Surely there's no rule against that."

"...Not... strictly..." Rutherford belabored himself. "But what of the event itself? '*Open Market Sale*?' Can you swear that such an occasion will be held in downtown Port Mauraisa, come Maypril, four years hence?"

"They sell things in the market there every day," Grover answered. "Stands ta reason they still will be." He raised his hand. "On me honor, I'll print the cancellation notice meself, if somethin' comes up."

"Hmm..." Rutherford contemplated, long and solemnly. Art's heart was pounding in his chest waiting for an answer. His consent certainly seemed quite dubious. Still, he hadn't turned them down straight away...

"You ought to know I am not a flexible man," the General made his answer. "Nor do I abide by flexible scruples. You have bent both to the very threshold of their breaking point here. That it is quite beyond the limits of my imagination to appreciate your wish to circulate this flyer is no help, either." Just as they were most hopeless, the General turned to them, a new light catching in his facets. "But... after all... it is a *very* great favor owed here.

Truly very, very great. So, I will propose this compromise: Let us remove the copies in ink, so that we may at least conform to a template."

Art suppressed a groan, rubbing a calloused thumb over calloused fingers. Those first few hundred flyers had been as much work as any... he hated to think of them going completely to waste. "That's really going to set us back. Do you think we'll still have enough flyers to cover the jungle?"

"My dear fellow, you haven't anywhere near that many to begin with," the General explained delicately. "This job, done properly, would take a whole flight of Bombers and tens or even hundreds of thousands of flyers."

Art did not suppress his groan this time. "Of all the lousy..." he cut himself off. "Well, what do we do now? We don't have time or cash to get this mass-produced."

The General started pacing again. "Then I'd suggest refining your target area, if that is at all possible."

Art and Grover exchanged looks. Grover shrugged. "He does glow in the dark."

Art snapped. "That's thinking." He looked back at Rutherford. "How about it, General? Feel like putting on a night raid?"

"Consider it done!" Rutherford elated. "We have been meaning to test our mettle after dark!"

Art didn't particularly like the sound of that, but it was really getting too late to have reservations now.

"...But first," the General went on, his tiny legs clinking as he went for the canvas bags, "we must sort."

The crew converged on the bags and had them overturned before Art could say, *"mrrrgh..."*

* * *

The Grand Flyer Sort went well enough. Grover and Art were naturally exempted from participating in any case, being both unqualified and subject to conflict of interest. Rarely more than half awake, Art did at least pay token attention to the proceedings for a few minutes. Though he had shared something of Deborah's experience seeing Clerks rifle through files, he'd never witnessed Postmen sorting mail. While, to the totally casual observer, it might have been just a blur of shuffling paper in either case, Art's skills of observation detected subtle differences. Firstly, Clerks were markedly faster. They effectively ate through whole stacks of documents with joyful enthusiasm. Postmen were still efficient in their own right, but almost deliberate… solemn, even… handling each flyer as if to cherish it for just the briefest of moments… before either resolving to drop it down into the muck and mire of the jungles, or rejecting it outright.

General Rutherford woke Art later to inform him that the deed was done. He lamented he had not realized at the onset that there might be flyers written up in all different colors… as, indeed, there turned out to be. But the deal had already been struck, and he was no more inclined to back out of delivering on his word than anything else. So the crayon flyers were loaded into their customized chutes. The rest were returned to Art and Grovers' possession – for what it was worth to them…

Then… it was back to waiting. Waiting for dusk… when the flight would commence…

* * *

"Awake! Awake, Mr. Mallard!" General Rutherford boomed. "Awake! The time has come!"

"*Mph,*" Art protested. "I think I'd rather sleep through it, if it's all the same to you."

"It most certainly is not!" the General exclaimed, his tone not at all confrontational, but very resolved nonetheless. "According to your own mission parameters, we shall be searching over an entire sea of trees for a single point of blue light. It will take all our sights trained on the ground, and even then, the odds are astronomically against us. But! We do not shy from the impossible task. We do not fail. In the name of all duty and honor, we *shall* not."

Art found himself involuntarily on his feet for the second time that day. "Yes, sir," he saluted. "How exactly do you want me to help?"

Rutherford pointed at an outcropped window on the port of the craft. "You and Mr. Grover will each man one of the old turret viewports. A Bombardier will join you in each. The Pilot and Engineer will observe through the main windscreen."

"And you?"

The General drew himself up. "I'll be there with them, manning the controls."

Art blanched. "You… fly? Isn't that what you have the Pilot for?"

"And yet hers is the keenest sight of all... with the possible exception of present company. I'd prefer that she focus on the search for your intended recipient." He whirled around with a flourish of his cape and made for the control perch. "And as neither she nor I has ever flown at night, I see no great disadvantage to my handling the controls in her stead."

Art sighed. "Whatever you say, General."

"Indeed," Rutherford agreed, pulling the control yaws in toward him with unseen force. "And so my word is given: Engage the engines, Mr. Perez!"

* * *

The takeoff could have been more terrifying, honestly. The Bomber had about a million directions it seemed to want to go in, and any one of them besides straight up felt a little too much like falling for Art's taste. He didn't really enjoy the view out the window, watching the ground retreat. Casually shifting his attention into the cabin, he didn't long linger on Grover, either, who was clearly horrified and looked more ghastly than ever. Instead, Art watched the crew, trying to imagine their tiled visages were projecting great confidence. All through the unsteady ascension, his stomach was jostled mercilessly, but he endured that well enough. Through no known fault of his own, Art seemed to have something of a sky-high nausea threshold...

"Contact!" the General called, and Art and Grover were nearly thrown from their seats as he leaned into the yaws. In a second the props throttled up with a strength that shamed a whole chain of drive cars from the trains of Jast-Madiir. Even so, as the craft gained momentum, Art did his best to convince himself he was merely on such a train, riding over a high bridge, as he'd experienced many times. An unbearably loud train, in this case... on the ricketiest bridge imaginable...

"This bucket of bolts sounds ready to shake apart!" Art felt obliged to mention.

"I'm going ta throw up!" Grover elaborated.

The General seemed to exchange looks with his crew, with each giving him a nod. Some silent consensus was reached between the Postmen...

"Initiating Code Green!" the General called. He yanked on the yaws...

The Bomber leapt into a steep, rolling climb. Art buried his claws into the contours of his seat while he tried to form some coherent objection. He had yet to arrive at any sufficiently meaningful verbiage by the time they were all inverted and plummeting – still anchored in their chairs by little more than a tangential force heretofore alien to the sum of Art's life experiences. But as he watched the trees careen for the viewport, the craft at last scooped itself back into a straight and level course. They were flying just as they had a moment ago – which Art now found an inexpressible relief.

"Just what in the Heck was that about!?" Art asked through heaves of air.

The General looked back. "Code Green! As in: Greenhorn! We've observed that a timely barrel-roll does wonders for the morale of first-time fliers!"

"*Barrel roll...*" Art repeated, still gasping. "Right. I suppose anything after one of those wouldn't seem so bad."

"I'm going to need a new handkerchief," Grover said, a thousand-yard-stare in his crazy eyes. Art soon smelled what he was talking about...

"Relax, now, gents," Rutherford instructed them, angling the craft for the jungles – an endless horizon of ruddy broccoli it seemed in the twilight. "And keep those seeing little orbs in your heads peeled! The search begins in earnest..."

* * *

Art did as instructed, looking out on all the broccoli till his head was spinning. The dreary day had dubiously arrived at a clear night, and even after the sun went out, light from the Other Worlds was adequate to lend eerie relief to the landscape below. Frankly, it was putting a damper on their chances... and their spirits. Any time they thought they saw what might be the faint blue glow of a Meduseldan, it would always turn out to be a glistening little creek, or something annoying like that. They flew for hours. They passed from one end of the jungle to the other, and back again, deep into the night. And as they went ever onward, the real magnitude of the area became ever clearer. They wouldn't be able to thoroughly sweep the whole thing in one night. Maybe not a week's worth of nights...

"This is hopeless," Art admitted at last. "I'll give it to the end of the night, but let's face it. Our goose is cooked."

"Speak for yerself, Boyo!" Grover protested. "Ya might be able to walk away from this emptyhanded, but I can't! It'll be me head if we don't find that Taltax!"

"Really gents, I don't know why you insist on having your drivel about life and death when so much greater things are already at stake here!" the

General put in. "It is true, we shall have to close the books on this stage of the mission soon enough. These contraptions can't fly indefinitely. But I shall return with a dozen more, should we fail this night! The message must reach its recipient! That goes beyond any favor owed. It is the very essence of our charge."

"I like your spunk, General," Art said, "but for me, it's do or die tonight. Otherwise, it'll be too late for my defense lawyer client to help his bug."

The General telegraphed a look at Grover, who shrugged. "First I've heard of it."

"How this entire errand does confound me," General Rutherford admitted. "Still, I am affirmed! If it is absolutely true that this *must* be done tonight, then it follows, absolutely, that it *shall* be done tonight."

Art snorted. "Well that sounds nice enough. But I don't..."

"Look there!" the Pilot Yvonne de la Mancha called out, pointing through the windscreen with one extended leg. Everyone crowded into the front viewport...

Sure enough, Art's eyes homed in on a ghostly point of blue light a ways ahead of them. As they were coming up on it, it showed no sign of suddenly broadening out to a stream, river, or other such thing. No, this time it remained a *point*...

"Well-espied, my dear lady!" Rutherford commended her. "I do believe you've found our mark! But let not the deciding vote rest with me. How read you this, Mr. Mallard? What do your investigator eyes see?"

Art squinted for all he was worth, and then some. To him, it was still just a little blue spot...

"Could be him," Art answered finally. "Or else a rock in the light of the Other Worlds." He shrugged. "Definitely the best lead we've had tonight. Whatever it really is, I'd say we dump some flyers on it."

"Outstanding!" Rutherford said, throttling way back. "Hurry with the chutes, my good fellows! We'll be over our mark by the count of five."

The First and Second Bombardiers scampered to their stations, delaying scarcely a moment before engaging the chutes in flawless unison. He couldn't possibly have heard it over the props, but Art's imagination treated him to the sound of the hundreds of flyers whipping about crisply in the night air, down to the nice sturdy ground below, where it would be plucked up by a rather perplexed Meduseldan linguist...

"The ammunition is spent, General," Romero Lautrec reported.

"Then let us hope we are successful," Rutherford sighed. It was a contented sort of sigh, Art thought… as if he knew they had indeed prevailed, even without any earthly way to be sure. "Where to now, gentlemen?"

"Take us back ta the hill, if ya please, General," Grover answered.

"So be it." He gently began to bring the aircraft around…

Art ran a hand over his narrow head, myriad levels of exhaustion whelming him. "This is as far as I've planned," he admitted to Grover. "I had a way we could try to flush him out. But now that we've given it a whirl, I don't have the first thought about how to nab him from here."

"Leave that to me, Boyo," Grover assured him. "I got an idea about where he might be comin' out of the jungle. Leastwise, I remember where he went in."

Art nodded. "Good enough for me."

* * *

There wound up being plenty of time for rest. Based on their best estimations about where they had made the drop and the maximum float speed of Meduselda, they gave him until the afternoon at the earliest. As evening fell, Art began to feel discouraged again…

But he needn't have worried. Before they could even see anything, huddled as they were by the jungle's edge, they began to hear the snapping of tiny branches… a volume of noise no animal had dared make all day long, but befitting someone like Jojojo, for whom the thought of being maimed or torn to pieces by roving killers in the jungle (sentient or otherwise) held no menace. Art and Grover took up silent stations opposite each other, waiting for their mark…

After what seemed a very long wait, the snapping sound finally abated… and sure enough… out floated a Meduseldan drone, smartly garbed for safari. Momentary disbelief afforded the unsuspecting Jojojo only a few feet of travel over the open plain, before he was blindsided and tackled to the ground in a canvas bag…

Chapter 11

"*Well, I'll be...*" Horus said, overcome with wonder.

"You'll be... what?" their distinguished guest inquired. "Your predicate has shed its direct object."

Deborah rolled her eyes. "Yup, definitely a linguist."

The Meduseldan in their midst turned to her, flashing excitedly and pointing at her with one of his numerous rulers. "And *you*, young lady, have misplaced your subject."

Art made room between puffs on his pipe for a quip. "Now you see what I went through getting him here."

"I see *some* of what you went through, at any rate," Horus said, trying to mind his sentence structure. "But I'm still reeling to imagine what it took to find him in the first place."

Art shrugged. "Same old sort of business as always." The linguist began to protest but Art quickly cut him off. "I know, I know... no subject or verb." He turned back to Horus, who was still beaming. "Anyway, what's the matter with you? If I didn't know better, I'd think you were surprised by my success."

"...Not at all," Horus replied – clearing his throat – tugging at his shirt collar, which suddenly seemed too tight. "I never had a moment of doubt."

Art gave him a look. "*Right...*"

Horus snickered nervously. "Alright... I confess: You've done the impossible. How did you manage it?"

"Mostly, he and his accomplice managed by employing strong-arm tactics and mean-spirited trickery," the linguist leapt in. "They coaxed me out of the jungle on a false pretense, then stuffed me in a bag!"

"...And that was just the easy part," Art continued. "First we had to make hundreds of flyers, then we had to spend all night flying around hoping to find a little blue speck of light to drop them on. We were just lucky we found the right speck."

"You may imagine my consternation," the linguist went on, "when some daft thing in the sky kept passing, making a beastly racket all night, disrupting the sleep of the Tribe I have been studying. Then, at last, when the thing had gone straight over us, we wound up doused in invitations to an infantile 'Open Market Sale'. The Tribe declined to go at once, of course.

But I must hand it to your objectionable friend, the private investigator Mallard. He had his wily way of drawing me back to civilization."

Horus turned to Art. "And what was that? What was at the 'market' that a Meduseldan linguist simply could not resist?"

"Nothing as such," Art explained. "It wasn't the content of the flyer we hoped would catch his attention. It was the *postage date*."

"The flyer asserted, 'Maypril 35th, year of the Static Era 9020'," the linguist chimed.

"Grover told me that our friend here was getting up there, age-wise," Art went on. "We decided our best gambit was to make him think he'd let time get away from him. Basically, we tricked him into coming out of the jungle to hurry up and get his research published before he turned 140 and bit the dust."

"That is *not* what you did," the linguist argued.

Art's ears flicked. "It wasn't?"

"No."

Art was at once beside himself. "Alright, wise guy, then suppose you tell us why you came out, if not because we tricked you."

"Oh, I don't mean to imply that you did not trick me. However, our mutual acquaintance Grover missed his estimate of my age, somewhat. The flyer was post-dated months later than I should rightly have expired." He threw his tentacles aloft with a brilliant flash. "I came back out of the jungle to announce to the world that I was immortal!"

Horus grinned. "Well, whatever the particulars of your being here," he extended his hand for a handshake, "it is a very distinct pleasure to meet you, Mr. Jojojo."

"It's pronounced, 'Jo-ho-yo'," Jojojo explained. Horus thought he heard Art groan.

"My apologies, sir," he said, continuing to hold his hand out. "...May we still shake hands?"

"We may indeed shake hands, but I believe it would be more courteous on my part if we did not do so. Don't forget that I am electrically charged."

Horus blanched. "Ah, yes."

"For the sake of formality, though, you may shake the other end of one of my rulers," Jojojo went on, extending the wooden measuring stick. Horus obliged, however silly it seemed.

"What are all those rulers for, anyway?" Deborah asked.

Art huffed. "You've been out of Claptrapanese class too long. Those rulers are for rapping knuckles."

The linguist whirled. "Dimly indeed do I grasp what 'knuckles' are... much less why I should rap them. These are merely the accessories of my trade; it is a matter beyond question or reason. But now, let us meet this Mantid client of yours, Mr. Templar. I grow weary of these inquiries, and I find I would prefer the company of someone who is more diligent in the execution of his grammatic conventions."

Horus absently twisted the hairs of his chin between his claws. "Goodness... my *client*. I've spent so much time worrying I'd never be able to speak with him. Now that it's possible... I find I can't even remember what to ask."

Deborah held up a notepad. "I've got all your questions here, Boss."

Horus smiled. He remembered, at least, that he'd never dictated the questions he had for his client. Even so, he was quite sure she had every one of them written down...

"Excellent," Horus said. "Let's go."

Jojojo sighed. "Another direct object goes by the wayside..."

* * *

The carriage ride to Civil HQ was an awkward one, characterized by silence. No one really wanted to speak, lest they be corrected. Deborah had the luxury of occupying herself with taking notes (or at any rate pretending to). Art, having already miraculously delivered on his end, excused himself from the trip altogether. That left Horus and Jojojo... sitting quietly, and without diversion. Finally, it proved too much for Horus. He didn't wish to be inhospitable... certainly no more so than they had already been, what with Art's little indiscretions of deception and kidnapping. Reluctantly, he drummed-up a conversation...

"So... you're a linguist," he began.

"Yes, I believe that fact was firmly established," Jojojo replied.

"That's true," Horus said shifting in his seat as he strained the chat forward. "I only mention it again because I'm curious... what languages are you fluent in?"

Jojojo tipped a ruler at him. "That is very bad form, Mr. Templar; you've ended a sentence with a preposition."

"You have my sincerest apologies," he said, already deeply regretting that he'd brought this on himself. It was made up for, somewhat, when he saw a wry grin tug at the corner of Deborah's jowl, her eyes not straying from her notepad...

"But to answer your question," Jojojo went on, "I have studied every droll little language you could suppose... from the quaintly juvenile to the very most uninspired, slapdash tongues imaginable." He reached into a safari bag and retrieved a large book, flipping through it. "For instance, in addition to my tribal studies, I have recently mastered the elocution of Temporal Sub-Othmarran."

"Temporal Sub-Othmarran?" Horus repeated.

"Yes, it is rather peculiar. Every word in the entire language consists of varying durations of the syllable 'Wah'."

"Sounds like quite the accomplishment."

Jojojo's arm-tentacles curled up in something approximating a shrug. "It was no extraordinary feat. Othmarran has an unfortunate tendency to bait one into splitting one's infinitives, but beside that lone trifle, I would say a half-wit could master it with little effort."

"You know, for a linguist," Deborah piped-up, "you seem pretty critical of languages."

Jojojo pulsed with blue light. "Oh, I'm sure you have no idea!" He waved toward himself. "Go on, one of you, and give me any language! I can describe it for you perfectly in one word!"

Deborah and Horus exchanged an unsure look. "Alright," Horus finally went along. "How about Elfish?"

"Ha!" Jojojo laughed. "Presumptuous."

"Despotopian?" Deborah offered.

"Technically, that is a *dialect*... though I am unsurprised at your confusion. Even so: Overbearing."

"Pantaeric?"

"Fickle."

Deborah put up her notepad and folded her arms. "Aren't there *any* languages you've learned to appreciate?"

"*Appreciate*!?" he asked, aghast. "Now why should I do a thing like that?"

They exchanged another look. "We just thought..." Horus began, "...that is, after all these years in the field, it seems like you would have at least developed some... shall we say, professional enthusiasm?"

"Oh, I am quite enthusiastic about the work I do, Mr. Templar – you needn't fret about that. My Dominion – the Taltaxikhomer Margaritamoarmonums – boasts all of the world's finest and most enthusiastic linguists. But you fail to properly characterize the joy we know in our work. We do not study other languages as if to revel in their peculiarities. Rather, we study them to learn their various faults and shortcomings."

"Would you care to explain why?"

"It is elementary. Each of the Seven Dominions of the Meduselda was created with its own language – the seven oldest tongues. But of those tongues, it was *ours* – Claptrapanese – which became common to all the Dominions... and to all civilized peoples known to have followed. That was no accident of fate. Ours was the language that rose to the top because it was the *finest* language – the most expressive, the best structured, the most tasteful and superlative. My studies, therefore, are aimed at building the body of proof – at showcasing the many ways that Claptrapanese is superior to all other traditions – written, spoken, and otherwise."

"I'd be willing to bet your years of studying Mantid linguistics hasn't unearthed anything to change your mind," Deborah ventured.

"You would win that wager. The language of the Tribes is a typically faulty one. Their subjunctive, for instance, leaves much to be desired."

"*The* language?" Horus asked. "But you've studied Tribes in Jast-Madiir, Maenea, and Despotopia, have you not? Do you mean to say they all share *one* language?"

"That is correct, Mr. Templar. I have discovered three distinct *dialects*, but only one *language*."

Horus perked up a bit at this. "Well, that's good news! I hadn't previously considered that the Tribes might have various enough languages that even *you* would not be able to speak with my client. But with your assurances that there is only one language, I suppose that's nothing to worry about."

Jojojo shook himself as if to disagree. "I cannot guarantee my knowledge of the Tribes is exhaustive, Mr. Templar. There may still be other languages I have not yet encountered... though, indeed, it is unlikely. Whatever the case, you may take comfort in this: Even were his tongue wholly unknown to me, still I am sure I could master basic communication within a couple of weeks."

Now Horus shook his head. "As remarkable as that would be, we have only a couple of *days*. The trial begins... the day after tomorrow..."

* * *

Horus and company fetched many a skeptical expression from the moment they entered the Police Department. Not the least skeptical was the Deputy Constable, all his features seeming to scrunch inward toward his mustache. Horus had seen this face before and knew it well by now. The idea that he had actually found a translator for the bug seemed so far removed from reality that Miloje clearly felt he was being deceived – though he couldn't put a finger on exactly where, how... or why. Worse yet, he was powerless to do anything but go along with Horus' demands and look surly about it...

As they finished filling out a pass for Jojojo, Miloje released them from his supervision into the thoroughly bruised hands of Captain Alexei, grumbling off into some other corner of the HQ building. Horus was privately relieved. He was sure his next stunt would be easier to navigate by the Captain than the Deputy Constable...

Alexei whisked the metal door to the glass holding cell open, gesturing in. "Here you are, lady and gents," he said. Horus, however, did not budge for the door, effectively bottlenecking the two others in his party. Alexei's chipper countenance began to droop as moments passed silently by.

"Aren't you going in, Mr. Templar, sir?" the Captain finally asked.

"Not this door, Alexei," Horus stated, firm but fair. "I'm going to ask that you let me *behind* the glass."

Alexei blanched. "You... you're asking to be put in with the bug?"

Horus shrugged. "It's not so unusual, is it? Attorneys often confer with their clients that way. It's certainly easier than trying to speak past a thick wall."

"But *maximum-security* clients?" Alexei objected. "Perhaps you've gained the means to speak with him, sir, but you've not yet learned anything about him... nor he about *you*. There's no telling how he might react. He might attack you."

Horus just grinned. "That's a chance I'm more than willing to take." He looked the still-harried policeman up and down. "As a man who frequently puts his own life and limb on the line, I hoped you would understand. Either way, you shouldn't try to restrict me in this, Captain. You don't have sufficient grounds."

"I… I don't?" Alexei protested weakly.

"No."

The Captain breathed through his nose. He stroked his chin. He looked all around, as if to be sure Miloje hadn't doubled back on them. "Very well, Mr. Templar… if that's really how you'd like it. Let me lead you round the other way…"

Even as Alexei began to show them down another bend in the hall, Horus stopped Deborah. "I'm sorry I failed to mention this part of my plan before," he said. "There could be some danger. The bug still has claws and mandibles, after all… and I did shoot at him once. Alexei's warnings aren't unfounded in that sense. If you're at all hesitant, please don't feel the need to follow us in." He searched her eyes with conviction. "I don't expect you to."

Deborah smiled fearlessly. "The little guy doesn't scare me. I have a clipboard, and I know how to use it."

Horus nodded. "I've no doubt. Very well… we'll accept the marginal risk together."

"Always."

* * *

The door clamped and clamored shut… locked down tight. Horus, Deborah, and Jojojo stood (or floated, as the case might be), opposite the cement-colored lump on the ground. After a few moments of study, Horus could see that his client's face was indeed turned at them… turned at *him*… so that he was front and center in both massive eye clusters. They had already given each other the stare-down many times by now… but with both barrier and restraints removed, this was naturally a whole new dynamic. Horus did his best to normalize it, inasmuch as he could project the same air as he had in their previous meetings. Speaking through Jojojo was one thing. He still wanted to relate some measure of his own earnest goodwill first, if he could…

"You make a better door than a window, Boss," he heard Deborah say behind him. It caused him a bit of shock to learn he had evidently, unconsciously positioned himself directly in the gulf between her and his client. So much for his projection. He was sending defensive signals he wasn't even registering…

"Sorry," he said, shuffling at least a little out of her line of sight. He cleared his throat. "The floor is yours, 'Jo-ho-yo'. Why not start out with some friendly greeting or other?"

"It's pronounced, 'Yo-jo-yo," the linguist corrected, even as he probed his safari bag. "Give me a moment while I retrieve my instruments..."

Presently, 'Yo-jo-yo' produced precisely that – *instruments* – dark little castanets. Before Horus had time to wonder, the linguist was clacking the little things together in his tentacles with an intricacy that was clearly conversational. The bug leapt to its feet in surprise – wings aflutter under their heavy covers. He chittered something quite brief, seeming unsure. Jojojo repeated his first pattern of castanet clicks. The bug responded, this time in a longer series of alien sounds.

"Ah my, how very interesting this is!" Jojojo said. "Your client seems to be of mixed dialects! Let me see now... I shall have to improvise a bit..."

He reached back into his bag and got out a set of spoons. Then he wove a new pattern on the castanets, even as he supplemented with tinny clunks from the spoons, which he held together, slapping them back and forth between a bend in one tentacle and another outstretched.

The bug's antennae bobbed sporadically, the whole creature seeming to come alight with energetic curiosity. He responded again to Jojojo's clicks with a string of his own.

"Castanets and spoons?" Deborah inquired.

"Yes, these are two of the dialects of which I spoke earlier," Jojojo explained. "Native Jast-Madiiran Mantid speech is most easily approximated by castanets. Mantids that once occupied Roemnar now inhabit both Maenea and parts of the Jast-Madiiran jungle band; theirs is the dialect of spoons. Oddly, I have found it most easy to converse with Despotopian Mantids using simple, 'click-clack, clickety clack' vocalizations."

"I'd love to hear all about it later," Horus said, as internally wound-up as the bug was. Procuring a translator had been a relief... seeing his client *respond* now was like magic. He didn't care to be bombarded with trade information at the moment. It was time to ***talk***, at last... "What is he telling you? What have you told him?"

"I gave him a rather elaborate hello. He asked me to repeat it, in sheer disbelief. I did. He has since asked me what the big furry friend of the terrible bird-woman is doing here, and whether you intend to try to blow him up again."

Horus flushed under his onyx coat. "Tell him I'm his defense attorney. Tell him... just tell him I want to help him."

Jojojo used his various implements to click, and the bug clicked right back – a rather defiant string, it seemed to Horus. "He has his doubts," Jojojo relayed. "He's on about the whole explosion thing again." He turned to Horus. "What exactly did you do to him?"

"I shot at him," Horus admitted. Jojojo tried to form another question but Horus waved him down. "...No time to explain. Tell him that my name is Horus Templar. Ask him for his."

Jojojo clicked the message. The bug looked back and forth between Jojojo and Horus, apparently deliberating whether to divulge his identity or not. Finally, he chittered his response...

"He says his name is Aphelo," Jojojo explained.

Horus nodded, grinning. *Aphelo*, he mused. One simple word that in a moment transformed his client from the everybug into an individual... the very thing Horus needed him to be, if he were to have any chance of success. Even as he tumbled the name around in his head – growing accustomed to it, noting how inexplicably fitting it was – Aphelo began to vocalize again... another long strand.

"What did he say?" Horus asked.

"He says that he's grown very tired of all the mixed messages he's been getting. He's grateful for the bandaging but doesn't understand why he's being terrorized and treated as a prisoner by all these strange and unsightly people. He expresses a very strong wish to leave."

Horus hurt for Aphelo, as he began to realize just how little the bug had understood the mess he was in from the start. His ears turned back with dismay, as he massaged the flanks of his snout between his eyes. "You'd better explain his predicament."

A very long and increasingly agitated exchange of clicks, clacks, and chitters ensued between Jojojo and Aphelo. Horus just rode it out, again able to do little besides try to appear composed for Aphelo's benefit. He was used to his clients at least having some appreciation for their odds. This time, the poor, unsuspecting little guy had spent weeks not even knowing for sure he was being held at fault. It was doubtless a lot to swallow...

"He says you need to get him off scot-free," Jojojo relayed finally. "He says his Tribe was sacked – that he should be there now, helping rebuild." Aphelo clicked a final appeal. Jojojo flashed with alarm. "He says he left a wife and egg-sack back home."

At that, whatever remained of morale promptly flew out of the room.

To get things moving again, Deborah ripped a sheet free from her notepad. "Here's those questions you wanted," she said, handing it to Horus.

He took it, scanning for some clincher he might have forgotten about. No such luck. Pertinent questions, all, but even with the most ideal answers, it would merely be the uncorroborated testimony of his client on his own behalf. To top it off, Horus had received final word from Primary Administrator Hihvnor the day before: There would be no intervention from the Inquisition. He was on his own. "*Right*," Horus sighed, snapping the paper up straight, trying to hold it out like it was a handful of aces. "Let's get started."

Chapter 12

"Court will come to order," Vizier Neferib declared, her voice echoing up to the furthest, darkest reaches of the amphitheatre. She *had* to say it, of course – as a matter of procedure – even though the entire venue was already gripped in quiet stillness. All gathered had arrived with time to spare, spending the last half-hour or so training themselves not to blink, lest they miss even an instant of the exotic and much-hated adversary being brought in from the jungles...

But the public had other reasons to be orderly. If the exhibition about to be put on before them was the proverbial carrot, *the Loge* behind them was the stick. Horus' cases had never brought him to the Royal Judicature before – this characteristically extravagant marriage of court and colosseum – but the Loge was notorious among the defense attorneys who'd known such misfortune in the past. 'The Pillbox,' they called it – a lofty enclosure at the back of the theatre, behind an opulent vanguard of seven enormous nacre-whale pearls arranged on a semicircle of golden stands – the sigil of the Czars and Czarinas given form. The box itself was not so glamorous, but still perfectly completed the desired effect. It was a thick and heavy enclosure with a wide window, beyond which everything was invariably shrouded by impenetrable blackness. It was a fine setup for the Czarina, to be sure. There was no way to tell, at any given moment, whether she was personally overseeing the trials convened in the nation's highest court, or not. And if there was one thing more unnerving than knowing she was there, it was not being *able* to know...

Theatrical – even gladiatorial – overtures of his surroundings aside, Horus did not consider himself entirely without good fortune here. The one potential imperfection in the Czarina's otherwise clutch, prefabricated execution drama was her choice of judge. Vizier Rashida Neferib was one of only three Viziers in the Archipelago; together, they comprised the Annex Tribunal – the highest international court in the region. Elevated as Neferib was, and not closely tied with any one state, the Czarina didn't exactly have her in her back pocket. Her conviction rate reflected this, hovering all the way down in the mid-eighties percentage range. Suffice it to say, there were many tougher judges – Lionel Ramesses, Bastet, Senahktenre – but none higher than a Vice-Vizier. The Czarina had apparently made the rather uncharacteristic tradeoff for clout at the expense of an exceptional track record. Horus was okay with that.

Even as he considered the Vizier, she stood. "Let the Trial of the Mantid commence," she declared. "Bring forth the accused."

Following the prompt, a bailiff in an executioner's mask rung a huge gong. Horus found this bit of showmanship rather gaudy, but he had to admit – it did catch him off-guard. While the reverberations continued to warble through the amphitheatre, a small, circular dais rose from beneath the ground, into the very epicenter of the arena. Here was Aphelo – bound foreleg, rear-leg, rearest-leg, and wing by some custom job that held him fast and upright. The frame of his full-body manacle was, in fact, expertly crafted to pose him in what must surely be his most menacing stance, his claw-arms extended in mid-strike. It was a far cry from what Horus had grown used to seeing over the past few weeks – a dejected, folded-up lump on the ground. Once the dais reached its full extension, it began to slowly turn, so that all gathered would have a chance to appreciate Aphelo's deadly appearance from every angle. Horus rolled his eyes. He began to feel more like a salesman at a new carriage dealership than a defense attorney...

"Does the prosecution have an opening statement?" the Vizier asked, after the awed murmuring of the onlookers had died down.

Hamilton Blackforest rose, carefully corralling his features to look solemn, when he might have otherwise appeared more sleek and predatory than the creature on trial. "We do, your Honor," he said, before moving to stand between Aphelo and the crowd...

"Jurors, witnesses, distinguished guests," he began. "We, the people of Jast-Madiir, find ourselves with an unprecedented opportunity this day. An opportunity, at last, to settle our nation's deepest grievances. An opportunity for *retribution*, many centuries overdue." He paused on this point, sharp fist tightly clenched, eyes sweeping over an enthralled populace. "It is in light of this that the State demands you bear in mind your *outrage*. Outrage at the loss of so many of your countrymen – those who have died in past wars with the Mantids... and those who will surely die in all such wars yet to be declared. Moreover, the Czarina implores you to consider an even *greater* outrage – the personal frustration she has known in defeat. Hers... and that of all of her predecessors. Let those atrocities guide your final judgment. I grant that none of you has ever – before this moment – laid eyes on our adversary." He leveled a condemning finger at Aphelo. "But *this*... this is their template... and the State will prove it. What you must do in response is beyond question. You must uphold the dignity of your country and your sovereign. I urge you: Do *not* miss this chance to tip the scales of justice in the proper direction... for it may never come again."

Blackforest returned to his seat. Horus was most impressed with his opening statement, if not daunted. He had, after all, spent many hours carefully crafting his own. And, as providence would have it, Horus had arrived at a new personal best in eloquence, right when it was most called for. Deborah and Art had agreed: It was the finest opening statement he'd ever written, by far. In fact, if there was one tool in his arsenal that had any chance of swaying the jury, then he knew this was it...

"Does the defense also have an opening statement?" Vizier Neferib asked. Horus grinned as he stood...

"We do, your Honor."

She gave him a probing look. "Is it very persuasive?"

A peculiar question, he felt, but he took it in stride. "Yes, extremely."

Neferib reached for her gavel. "In that case, the Court waives the defense's statement."

Horus blinked as her gavel clacked against the desk. He sat down. Perhaps her reputation for leniency was exaggerated after all...

"The prosecution may call its first witness."

Blackforest once again stood and faced the arena. "I call Doctor Nokkaeru to the stand."

Horus turned to watch as the Doctor rose from her perch. He was fastidious at making a careful study of witnesses, as they were called forward... though in this case it made little difference. Even if he had reason to think a mainstay of the SAPD's extended family would have anything to hide in a case like this, there was no way for him to read it in her alien composure, or her veiled face...

Still, looking into the crowd, he did notice something of import. He noticed a most concerning lack of blue glowiness. Further examination seemed to prove it – his key witness was *missing*!

"Where the devil is 'Yo-jo-yo?'" Horus whispered hoarsely at Deborah.

"Not 'Yo-jo-yo," she responded. "It's 'Ho-yo-jo' now."

"Ho-yo-jo? Since when?"

"Since the last time he corrected me, naturally. But either way, he's not here yet. He was still going over field notes with Grover when I left the office... said he might be a little late."

"*Late*? To the Royal Judicature? Does he realize how serious that is?"

She shrugged. "Probably."

Horus sighed... court had only just convened, and the few things he had going for him were already unraveling. "Well, so long as he shows in time to be called."

About the time they finished quietly conferring, Nokkaeru was sworn-in and perched on the witness stand. A bailiff with an easel came forward as well. Once the tripod legs were set up, the bailiff withdrew. Blackforest closed in...

"Now, Doctor," he started, folding his hands behind his back. "Would you please explain to the Court the nature of your association with the defendant?"

"The Mantid had injuries when it was brought into custody. I was summoned by the St. Argonsburg Police Department to administer treatment, as I often am when local medicine proves grossly inadequate."

"Very good, Ms. Nokkaeru," Blackforest nodded. "Now, will you also carefully explain what special qualifications you possess that made you the obvious choice to treat the bug's injuries?"

The Doctor was haughtily silent for a moment. "As I have just indicated, my medical knowledge – both in breadth and depth – far exceeds anything otherwise available in this unprepossessing country... though it does not bother me to repeat it."

Blackforest managed a diplomatic snicker. "That's not precisely what I was referring to. Rather, I would like you to explain, in your own words, the unique knowledge your people have concerning Dire Mantids."

"Ah, yes," she nodded. "You refer to our successful campaigns against them, in wars of old. We gained very extensive knowledge of their anatomical structure during this time, being afforded the benefit of their fallen for examination."

At this, Blackforest threw a cover off the easel, revealing a medical chart. "I show you now this diagram. Is it familiar to you?"

"Yes," she admitted, sounding a bit crestfallen. "It is an enlargement of a Dire Mantid physiological study from my own records – begrudgingly surrendered to your policemen."

"And you – the foremost expert available to us – would accept this diagram as the authority on said physiology?"

"I would. It is the diagram I used in my administration of treatment."

"You would swear, then – under oath – that the defendant perfectly conforms to this definitive diagram of Dire Mantid anatomy?"

"...No."

Every heart present skipped a beat. Every heart, that is, except for Blackforest's...

"Would you please repeat your answer, Doctor... and kindly elaborate?"

"You asked me if the defendant *perfectly* conformed to the diagram. He does not. However, that is not to be wondered about. The variances are really quite minor, and only tend to reinforce that the defendant's heredity is not precisely Roemnari."

"And what conclusion does this lead you to, Ms. Nokkaeru?"

"It leads me to suspect that the defendant is largely, if not entirely, of a breed native to Jast-Madiir."

"Objection," Horus called out. Blackforest shot him a look before making his own appeal to the judge...

"Your Honor, the defense has no grounds to impeach the conclusion of an expert witness. Or, does he wish to waste the Court's time, while I parade out the Doctor's extensive credentials?"

"The expert opinion of the witness is immaterial, when her conclusion is inherently prejudicial," Horus argued. "The defense stipulates that the Doctor has grounds to believe the defendant is not pureblood Roemnari. But she must admit that her people made no effort to catalogue the genetic variances of Maenean, Despotopian, and Jast-Madiiran Mantids. Her assertion that my client is native to this island is thus circumstantial – a conclusion drawn solely from the fact that he was found here. She cannot corroborate her conclusion with further evidence."

Vizier Neferib took a moment to think. "This is a matter of some sensitivity," she admitted. "Does the defense suppose he can, by further examination of the witness, thoroughly impeach her conclusion?"

"At least, I should be able to prove reasonable doubt," Horus answered.

"Very well," Neferib declared. "Let the prosecution's line of questioning be suspended, while we sort this out."

Blackforest turned, looking thoroughly disgusted. After a moment, however, he grinned, gesturing Horus toward the stand. "Your witness... for the moment," he said. Horus accepted the toothy invite...

"Now, Doctor," Horus began, "I couldn't help noticing a set of wings on this diagram. Tell me, does my client also have wings? Or is this one of the 'minor variances' you spoke of earlier?" He had hoped his playful sarcasm might win enough favor with the audience for some snickers, but no such luck. Not when the Czarina might be watching...

"Your client most certainly has wings," she answered.

"Ah, but are those wings sufficient for flight? Or would my client, at best, be an accomplished jumper?"

"An adult male Mantid, such as this, is indeed capable of sustained flight."

"So then, you admit it is possible that he came here, of his own volition and power, from a neighboring island?"

"It is possible," she admitted.

"Your Honor," Blackforest appealed, "surely the mere *possibility* of the defendant flying to Jast-Madiir prior to his capture doesn't constitute *reasonable* doubt! What evidence does Mr. Templar present that would make that narrative plausible? What could we reasonably suspect would possess him to pick up one day and fly here from Maenea or Despotopia?"

Horus did something uncharacteristic in this moment. "The aforementioned injury," he asserted, even returning to his desk. "I have brought my own enlargement, Doctor Nokkaeru." He retrieved it, putting it over Blackforest's diagram. "Can you identify it for the Court?"

"Objection!" Blackforest cut in. "This is all highly irregular! Does the Court intend to permit the defense such latitudes as to introduce his own exhibits before I've even finished with my first witness?"

The Vizier shrugged. "If the visual will aid in the clarification of this point, I see no reason to withhold it. You may still stamp your own exhibits according to procedure, even if his is currently covering yours up."

"Thank you, your Honor," Horus nodded. "Please, Doctor Nokkaeru... would you identify this enlargement?"

"It is a copy of my own personal sketch of the Mantid's principal injury."

"You explained to me privately the nature of this injury. Can you relate that to the Court at this time?"

"The wound is consistent with a raptorial foreleg attack from a larger Mantid specimen."

"Why would the defendant be attacked by another Mantid?"

"Inter-tribal warfare among Mantids is all-but continuous. They drive each other ever back and forth in petty territorial battles."

"So it is possible, then – even *plausible* – that my client was driven from his own settlement in such an attack?"

"That would be my interpretation of events, yes."

"Is it not, then, every bit as possible that he was driven away from some home in Maenea or Despotopia as from one here, in this land?"

"It is not."

Horus was momentarily dumbstruck again. That was *not at all* what he wanted to hear. He hesitated even to ask his next question, but he had no choice...

"Why not?"

"The *extent* of the injury in question. The creature could never have survived such a sustained flight, thusly damaged. He would have bled out in the effort."

Horus didn't peer back at Blackforest, but he could feel the DA's look of glee burning into him. His insides were on fire anyway. He *knew* better... because he *had known* better. He *had known* the attack didn't drive Aphelo on an island-hopping retreat, and thus should never have been so audacious as to try to distort the facts to say so. *How impulsive! How foolish...*

"I see," Horus managed. He heard Blackforest stand...

"If I may, your Honor, I think the prosecution can afford to concede the *possibility* – at least, for the moment – that the defendant may have immigrated here at some point. Though I dare say the defense seems to have done my work for me, showing how unlikely that narrative is. May I be allowed to continue my line of questioning now?"

"Yes, I believe that is in order," the Vizier said. Horus returned to his seat, deeply humiliated, but more ready for a fight than ever. *This isn't the last round,* he reminded himself...

Blackforest returned to the front, coolly flipping back to his own diagram. "Just a few more questions, Doctor. Since we cannot, at this time, establish certainly the national origin of the defendant, I ask you this: Can you still swear, beyond any shadow of doubt, that he *is* a Dire Mantid, and no other insectoid subspecies – intelligent or otherwise – that the Creators may have fashioned?"

"Yes," she said. "As far as his species goes, this is most certainly a member of the Dire Mantid race, with which your nation has long warred."

Blackforest smiled horribly. "Very good. Now, as to the bug's flight to the spot where he was found... how long do you make the journey, Doctor? Just how far could a Mantid with his injuries fly, in your estimation?"

"I make it five miles, at most."

"Thank you." He turned and went for his seat. "Your witness again, Mr. Templar."

Horus stood, approaching the easel. "My examination will be brief, since we have already established that the injury to my client was not incurred from any skirmish with Jast-Madiiran soldiers."

The Vizier pointed at Horus, a look of warning in her eye. "Do not editorialize your own questions, Counselor," she advised. "If you wish to establish a fact duly, you should illicit it from your witness in the proper context."

Horus cleared his throat, as he flipped to his wound enlargement again. "Very well. Then I ask you this, Doctor: Did you find any markings whatsoever on my client that would suggest he'd ever been in a fight with one of ours? Any scars from sword, bayonet, or other forged weapon?"

"No indeed," the Doctor replied.

"You were not surprised by the lack of such evidence when we discussed my client privately. Please tell the Court the reason you gave me."

"I indicated to you that the males of Dire Mantid culture do not serve as fighters. The females are much larger and more formidable."

There were murmurs in the crowd. Horus nodded, even managing a weak grin. "Thank you Doctor. No further questions." He sat.

"A few questions on redirect, your Honor," Blackforest interjected. "Miss Nokkaeru, you've just indicated that the morphology of male and female Mantids differs substantially."

"It does."

"So then, the diagram you used – it must have been of the male physiology?"

"Yes."

"How, then, were your people able to make studies of male specimens? Were they quite docile creatures? Did they surrender themselves peaceably to your warriors?"

"No. At no point were we able to take living prisoners – female or male. When pressed, the men fought or fled, in proportion to their ability."

"Then let me put a finer point on it: Are you aware of any facts to suggest that male Mantids are anything besides entirely complicit with the fighting efforts of their women?"

Nokkaeru shook her head. "Indeed I am not."

Blackforest returned to the easel one last time, snatching away Horus' diagram... followed by his own. "Thank you, Doctor – that will be all," he said, bringing the diagrams to the Court Clerk's desk. "Here we are – State's, and *defense's*, exhibits-A."

"You may step down," Neferib advised Nokkaeru. "Let the prosecution call his next witness."

"I call Sgt. Ivanovic to the stand."

* * *

"No, he wasn't very feisty when we first picked him up... but you have to consider the shape he was in," the Sergeant explained.

"Exactly what shape was that, Sgt. Ivanovic?" Blackforest asked.

"He'd been bandaged and fed by the people that found him... the Monroes, that is. But he was still weak and dazed. It wasn't until long after we had him in the bag that he really started thrashing."

"So you would say, then, that the defendant violently resisted his arrest?"

"Objection," Horus called. "My client does not know Claptrapanese. At no point could the soldiers have articulated to him that he was under arrest."

"Your Honor," Blackforest protested. "At no point thus far has any examination revealed that the defendant does not speak Claptrapanese. Mr. Templar refers to a fact not yet in evidence."

Vizier Neferib turned to face Horus. "You know you cannot introduce facts that way, Counselor." She clacked her gavel. "Objection overruled."

Drat, Horus thought.

"You were saying, Sergeant?" Blackforest rejoined.

"I was about to say yes, the defendant certainly put up a nasty fight."

"Very good, sir," Blackforest said, returning to his easel, apparently ready to reveal some new chart. He flipped a page over the back, displaying a map. "There is another line of questioning I wish to pursue. I show you now this map of central Jast-Madiir. Tell me, Sergeant, do you have knowledge of the location where the defendant was first discovered?"

"Yes... I was shown the spot by Mrs. Monroe." He scooted up to the edge of his chair, reaching out and pointing. "It's right... *there*. That red dot."

As this was happening, Horus found himself suppressing an objection. By all rights, it ought to have been Michelle Monroe testifying to this location, since it was she who found him there. He found it most curious that Blackforest would try to use a secondary source to establish this fact when he'd already brought the Monroes all the way to St. Argonsburg... for this very trial. Strange – and improper – as it was, Horus wasn't about to call him out on it. He remembered well the plight of the Monroes, and didn't want to be the one to call them forward, lest their inevitable perjury be on his conscience...

As it turned out, though, things were soon taken out of his hands...

"Hold there, Mr. Blackforest," Vizier Neferib called. "Something is amiss. We have Mrs. Monroe here to indicate the site where she found the Mantid. To introduce this fact through the Sergeant is not best evidence."

Horus couldn't help noticing Blackforest's ears fold out with unease.

"My apologies, your Honor," he answered. "I merely wanted to avoid needlessly recalling this witness to establish another fact. I can have Michelle Monroe corroborate the location in future testimony."

The Vizier ran clawed fingers down her whiskers. "I wonder at this... *reverse chronology*... you seem to enjoy calling your witnesses in. But on your assurance of corroboration, I will permit you to continue this line of questioning..." she looked over at Horus, "...unless the defense sees fit to object."

"No objection," Horus said.

"Very well. Continue, Mr. Blackforest."

"Thank you, your Honor." Blackforest returned to the map, producing a compass from within his suit jacket. He lined the compass up against the scale, then, with the point set on the red dot the Sergeant had indicated, he drew a green circle all the way around. "Now, according to the testimony of Doctor Nokkaeru, the defendant would have to have begun his flight somewhere within this five-mile radius."

"I'd say that adds up," Ivanovic nodded.

"Now, we come to another exhibit, acquired by special permission," Blackforest said as he reached behind the easel and flipped yet another page over. "Here is another map of the same region, which has already been stamped with the location of the defendant and the five-mile radius." He indicated numerous blue arrows, spanning roughly three times the radius of the green circle and extending beyond it both east and west, if not reaching quite halfway through it. "Could you tell the Court the significance of these arrows, Sergeant?"

"I can. The arrows are troop deployments. This map is marked up to match the battle-plans for the most recent campaign against the Mantid Tribes. A squad of soldiers would have advanced along each of those arrows."

"How interesting," Blackforest commented slyly. "I wonder how you account for the fact that these deployments just happen to align so well with the possible origin points of the defendant. Would you say it was mere coincidence?"

"No more coincidental than the Monroes doing their work in that part of the jungle," the Sergeant shrugged. "It's not so dense along that thirty-mile stretch. The leaves are thinner... there's better visibility. We've sent more campaigns through that area in the last century than any other entry point."

Blackforest nodded. "Thank you, Sergeant. I think that will be all."

As the witness changed hands, and Blackforest went on to have his new exhibits stamped, Horus folded his arms, giving the Sergeant a rather openly disapproving look. "Regarding my client's alleged resistance... I wonder, Sergeant, do you speak Despotopian?"

The Sergeant huffed. "Not a word of it. Why?"

"Well, suppose a troop of Despotopians were to come along and stuff you in a bag. Would you have me believe you wouldn't squirm or flail around at all?"

"Nope," the Sergeant grinned. "I would peacefully submit to their authority."

"I'm sure," Horus nearly growled. "No further questions."

Just as she might have dismissed the witness, the Vizier was approached by a bailiff. She turned an ear to him, receiving a hushed message. Then she nodded, sending the bailiff hustling for the entryway to the performance level. Neferib stood in address...

"There has been a disruption. A witness for the defense has arrived late. The Court will remain orderly as he is brought to account."

Horus shrunk over his desk, resting his head on one hand. At this point, it was hard not to feel two inches tall. Where he failed to humiliate himself, his witnesses were doing it for him...

The bailiff returned, a familiar Meduseldan in a safari hat floating slowly behind. "I apologize for my tardiness," he called to the Court, his voice filling the space expertly. "I was regrettably detained with other questioning. But rather than be displeased with me, consider instead that you ought to be grateful, for I have helped to greatly advance the scope of the xenobiological sciences."

The Vizier remained standing, looking quite unimpressed. "We do not concern ourselves with such things here. Your late arrival cannot be excused." She extended her gavel toward the table below. "I am sorry, but you will have to be executed at once..."

"One moment, your Honor!" Horus implored her, just as her gavel might have clacked. "The offender here is my key witness... I beg the Court's indulgence that I be allowed my questions before his execution."

Neferib folded her arms at him. "We have already endured numerous irregularities in the brief course of this trial. Why should I permit another?"

"It's really no bother," Jojojo interjected. "You may certainly deal with me as you see fit, Vizier. I can just as easily appear for questioning afterwards."

Not for the first time, Horus wished the linguist would put a sock in it. The pomp and circumstance of his execution could take *days*. By then, the trial would be over...

"If I may be so bold, your Honor," Blackforest said, rising from his own seat. "The State would greatly value its chance to cross-examine the supposed translator the defense seems to have conjured in the eleventh hour."

"*Supposed*, did he say?!" Jojojo protested.

"At any rate," Blackforest continued, "if Mr. Templar is so desperate for his chance to effectively submit his client's own testimony before this court, then I'm more than willing to let him."

Neferib examined Blackforest for a moment. She sat back down. "Very well. If you are both resolved on this course, I will permit the witness to be called by the defense now." She struck the table. It was done... even as Horus' gut sank with second thoughts. *Saved by Blackforest*... he mused. *That can't be good*...

Chapter 13

After a moment of incredulity, the court officer met Jojojo by the witness stand, preparing to swear him in...

"This oughta be good," Deborah whispered sideways at Horus. He wasn't immediately sure what she meant, until he considered what the process of swearing him in would entail...

"State your name, please," the court officer instructed Jojojo.

The linguist hesitated.

"...Well, suppose *you* say it first, and I correct you."

The officer raised a brow, but belabouredly checked his list of names. "It says here your name is... Jojojo."

"It's pronounced, 'Jo-yo-yo'," he explained.

"Yo-yo indeed," Deborah whispered again.

The officer continued. "Do you swear to tell the truth, the whole truth, or whatever portion of the truth best expedites the final ruling of this court, so help ye Creators?"

"I do so swear."

"Please take the stand."

Horus approached. "Let us begin with some meaningful context. Would you please explain to the Court the nature of your association with my client?"

"I was forcibly abducted to facilitate your communication with him," Jojojo replied.

"Yes," Horus agreed. "And, why was it necessary for us to enlist your help with this?"

"Simply, your client does not speak Claptrapanese... nor do you speak his language. In fact, it is a tongue unknown to any in the civilized world, beside me."

Horus looked back at Sgt. Ivanovic as he continued his line of questioning. "Would you say, then, that my client was quite unaware of the reason for his forcible transport to St. Argonsburg?"

"Oh yes... he was most unhappily surprised to learn the reason, as you'll recall."

Horus watched the Sergeant grimace and look down at the floor. He returned his focus to Jojojo. "We questioned him rather extensively about his knowledge of Humans, didn't we?"

"Yes we did, for what little he could reveal."

"Had he so much as *seen* a Human, prior to his encounter with Michelle Monroe?"

"No."

By now, Horus was pacing the floor thoughtfully. "And what of his Tribe's history of warfare with Humans? What was he able to relate about that?"

"He said he had never really bothered about who his Tribe was fighting at any given time. He said he would have to ask his wife."

"How very menacing," Horus quipped. "What more can you tell me about the defendant himself? His lifestyle? What are some of the grisly details?"

"He's quite the sedentary homebody, by all accounts. His interests include long naps and sleeping in. Though he expected things to pick up quite a lot, when his eggs hatch."

"Would it be a stretch, then – in your opinion – to describe the defendant as a hardened adversary of this, or *any* state?"

"Yes," Jojojo answered, flashing with profound agreement. "He harbors no obvious ill-will toward anyone."

"Very good," Horus nodded, returning to his desk. About the time he reached it, he looked back over his shoulder. "One more question, if I may. The defendant: What is his name?"

"His name is Aphelo."

Horus nodded again. "Thank you. That will be all." He returned to his seat in a smooth motion... though inside, he was locking up... dreading to discover how Blackforest was about to turn this moral victory inside-out...

Sure enough, as he drew himself up, the DA looked deviously pleased. "Well, first of all, thank you for finally joining us, my good Taltaxikhomer Margaritamoarmonum."

Jojojo harumphed. "If you know my Dominion, you ought not to go questioning my ability as a translator. We boast all the world's greatest linguists – of which I'm surely not the least."

Blackforest twitched slightly, a tiny chink momentarily taken out of his self-satisfied demeanor. "My mistake. But I wonder if..."

"...I am fluent in 308 means of communication, including contemporary and archaic languages, dialects, and codes."

Blackforest nodded uncomfortably. "That is most impressive. However..."

"...I take special pains not only to master the diction and syntax, but elocution as well. In particular, I have won wide acclaim for my performance of Elfish verse."

"Fascinating, sir, but really..."

"...You must permit me a demonstration..."

...Jojojo made a noise like clearing his throat, and before Hamilton could make further protest...

"*Phloom*."

For a time, the world seemed to stop. Only when Horus became conscious of his need to take air through the quivering lump in his throat did he begin to wrest himself free of the spell Jojojo had woven of pure, poignant emotion. Never in all his days of enjoying the best of St. Argonsburg's highbrow culture had he heard such a flawless recital of F. Presbyt McNolte's most cherished Elfish epic ballad. Never had he experienced so sublimely its nuanced subtleties – cautionary yet tender – evoking the agonies of age and decline, the rapture of rebirth... and the tranquil aroma of thinly-chopped cucumber on a cold spring evening. Granted, Horus didn't know Elfish, but so lyrical was the poem that its effect on the soul could hardly be mitigated. And he could not have been the only one that felt so. As Horus looked out through misty eyes upon all gathered, he saw that none was unmoved. Some openly wept.

"Thank you, Mr. Jo-yo-yo," Blackforest muttered at length, his eyes solemn as he tried to choke back the true extent of his gratitude.

The Vizier was the next to clear her throat. "Perhaps... you ought to get on with your examination now, Mr. Blackforest," she gently implored him.

Blackforest shook himself. "Yes... of course." He tugged his suit jacket as he closed in on the witness stand, killer instincts slowly reclaiming him from the depths of poetic reflection. "You have indeed proven, sir, your mastery of language... beyond any conceivable reservation."

"That is correct," Jojojo assented.

"However..." Blackforest began, "...I could not help noticing that your testimony hinged on a range of assertions unrelated to that field. You ventured your own assessment of the defendant's character. Tell me... how long have you known him?"

Jojojo flashed uncomfortably. "Two days."

"*Two days*," Blackforest recounted. "Hardly a lifelong friendship. But perhaps you have some qualifications in psychological profiling you'd like to tell us about?"

"I... erm... am not classically schooled, I'm afraid..."

"And what can you offer to corroborate the defendant's testimony on his own behalf?"

"Nothing, I suppose."

"You also testified that the defendant did not at first understand the conditions of his arrest. Tell me this: did he relate his narrative about being a docile homebody *before* you explained why he had been incarcerated, or *after*?"

"It was after," Jojojo admitted at length.

"How about his insistence that he'd never seen a Human?"

"...After."

Blackforest pulled back, pensively resting the ends of his fingers together. "Now, this next question may prove difficult. Suppose it was *you* on trial for war crimes against a Human nation. And... though it may strain your imagination... suppose you had a strong self-preservation instinct. Wouldn't you – in that situation – be inclined to make people believe you were harmless? Wouldn't you find it convenient to deny any knowledge of your Tribe's wars with Humans?"

"I suppose... I would... yes."

Getting the answer he wanted, Blackforest leaned in, clutching the railing in his claws, obviously preparing for a culminating question. Horus braced for the knockout blow...

"A final point, sir. The defense has tried to cast some doubt on whether this Mantid is native to Jast-Madiir. But tell me this: in your studies, have you discovered any linguistic artefacts peculiar to different regions? Accents, vernacular... perhaps even distinct *dialects* or *languages*?"

Here we go... Horus despaired.

"I have discovered three distinct dialects," Jojojo admitted, not seeming to appreciate at once the minefield he was being led into...

"And, which dialect does the defendant speak?"

Finally, Jojojo caught up with the situation. "He... he is a rather interesting case... he demonstrated mixed conventions..."

"*Which* conventions?"

Jojojo pulsated brightly with hesitance. "Roemnari, for one."

Blackforest nodded. "Interesting... considering Roemnari Mantids will have been displaced for centuries. And... the other?"

"...Jast-Madiiran."

The crowd muttered its astonishment. Neferib clacked a warning to maintain order. Blackforest repositioned himself astride Aphelo...

"There you have it, your Honor. The State has demonstrated definitely the defendant's membership in the Dire Mantid species... his immediate proximity to past campaigns, and... finally... his lifelong residence in this country. It has thus eliminated any reasonable doubt that the defendant belongs to a Tribe with which we have warred – not once, but many times in the past. The State asserts that his mere agency with such a Tribe makes him answerable to its aggression. The State moves that the defendant be bound over for war crimes, up to and including the highest applicable charge – Defamation of the Crown. Finally, the State rests its case."

Blackforest turned triumphantly for his seat. But before he could reach it, the Vizier stopped him...

"Just a moment, Mr. Blackforest. Did you not assure me that you would call Michelle Monroe forward, to corroborate the site where she found the defendant?"

Not for the first time, Blackforest seemed to diminish at the mention of the Monroes. "So I did," he laughed nervously. "It seems I got carried away. But I'll be happy to amend my mistake."

"See that you do. I cannot permit you to rest until you have fulfilled your obligations." She backed herself up with her gavel for good measure. "Let this witness be dismissed to his execution." A bailiff led Jojojo away...

A bit lethargically, Blackforest looked up and out into the court. "I call Michelle Monroe to the stand."

* * *

"Mrs. Monroe, you were the one to first discover the defendant, were you not?"

So this is Mrs. 'Mich' Monroe, Horus thought. She didn't look like a seasoned huntress of prize animals, eyes wide with fear she couldn't conceal. But it was hardly any wonder why. She had spent the whole day variously expecting to be called up for testimony and, occasionally, being given reason to expect she might not have to. Horus remembered well the capital offense that she herself was trying to hide. Art had pieced it together easily enough, and no doubt that leant to her anxiety. Her being called to testify had, apparently, been inevitable. To an otherwise honest person, the discovery of her secret must now seem equally inevitable...

"Yes," she answered, searching the arena for some comfortable spot to anchor her gaze.

Blackforest approached his easel once again, indicating the map of central Jast-Madiir. "I show you now this map." His voice was notably gentle and subdued. "I am pointing now to a red dot on the map. Can you verify that this is the spot where you made the discovery?"

She nodded. "Yes, that is the spot."

"Very good, Mrs. Monroe." Blackforest turned to the Vizier. "The State rests."

Neferib folded her arms, shook her head. "Really, Mr. Blackforest, I am surprised at you."

Hamilton tilted his head. "Your Honor?"

"The police statement of this witness is known to me. Apparently, I remember it better than you do. There is a point of great relevance which you have neglected..." She turned toward Michelle. "Now, Mrs. Monroe, it is understood that in the process of discovering the defendant, you incurred injury. Explain the nature of this injury to the court."

Here it was. Once again, though she had nearly got by without doubling-down on her lie, she was at last put up to it, with no further recourse...

"The defendant..." she began weakly. "He... he swiped at me with his claw."

More awed muttering from the throng.

"There, Mr. Blackforest," the Vizier stated. "You may now add proof of hostile intent to your case. But in the future, I strongly advise you not depend on the judge to supplement your efforts." She clacked her gavel and searched out Horus. "Commence your cross-examination, Counselor."

Horus stood, almost by reflex. He found himself studying Mrs. Monroe... weighing his options. He knew he could rebuff the 'hostile intent' of his client. It would be a simple matter of using demonstrable facts to reveal the *truth* – a nearly irresistible course of action for an attorney. The consequences for Mrs. – and Mr. – Monroe *would* be grim... but not undeserved, under the law of the land. They were guilty of dereliction of duty... and now, of perjury. And, after all, Horus' first obligation was to his *client*. Yes, even as he locked eyes with Michelle, it was perfectly clear what he ought to do now...

"No questions."

Horus sat back down, even as he watched Michelle slump in the witness stand, relieved at last. Somewhere behind him, he felt Mitchel Monroe do the same. Though he had, in essence, betrayed his duty and his client, Horus was glad. Even before the alleged 'swipe' came to light, Blackforest had crafted an air-tight case. To call the Monroes out now would only have meant condemning two more people...

"The witness may step down," Neferib said, before returning her gaze to Horus. "Does the defense also have a case to present?"

Horus blanched. "We do your Honor." It was all-but a bald-faced lie, but he had no policy against blatant deception for the purpose of buying time. With both the doctor and the linguist already thoroughly picked apart by Blackforest, Horus' only remaining recourse was to put his own secretary on the stand and introduce her account of his musket experiment into evidence... surely a failing last-ditch maneuver. More time was no assurance of a better idea... or *any* new ideas for that matter, whether better or worse. But it was, at least, *something* he might still be able to buy his client. "However," he went on, "we ask that the Court recess, until the following evening."

Neferib winced. "On what grounds?"

Deborah waved Horus over, whispering in his ear as he angled it toward her. "Inclement weather," Horus repeated aloud, as mystified as anyone by the reason he gave...

Neferib looked up doubtfully, turning a palm out as if to check for raindrops. It *was* an open amphitheatre... but the sky was clear, and the air still...

"Curious..." Neferib said. Horus ground his teeth, waiting for her to call his bluff...

"...Even so, perhaps we *ought* to adjourn for the night. We have had the prosecution's case today; let us have the defense's tomorrow. And let what weather may come in the meantime."

She struck the table.

As the sound of people dispersing grew to a dull roar, Horus sighed deeply, watching as poor Aphelo was retracted back underground. Despite his best intentions, and everything he could do, it was all-but certain now: Some time very soon, they'd be putting him underground for good...

Chapter 14

Art found himself once again standing at the end of the ramp – the one leading precariously up to the crew compartment of General Rutherford's postal bomber. His arrival here was timely – on time for the send-off, but too late to help load up all the cheap goods Grover had amassed over his last few days in Jast-Madiir. Art watched as Madeline toted the final, enormous shipping box into the rear of the craft, marveling at her carrying capacity...

About this time, Grover himself stepped out of the shadows. It was a full hour since sundark, and clouds had begun slowly rolling in, pulling a thin veil over the light from the Other Worlds. It was a mopey night, and getting mopier...

"Come to see me away then, Boyo?" Grover called out as he approached the ramp. Art was a firm believer in warm, heartfelt good-byes, and so called back with all due regard for his newfound friend...

"You betcha." Art examined Grover, sensing some of the mopiness of the night in him. "How did things go? Did you get some decent notes out of that linguist after all?"

"Aye," Grover laughed half-heartedly, "but I had ta pluck them out from quite a lot o' white noise." He held out a notebook. "There's enough sciencey stuff in here to satisfy the journal, I've no doubt."

Art nodded affirmingly. "Should be a nice homecoming, then."

Grover looked past him... his own nod was unsure. "...In a way..."

Art's ears folded back. "Still not sure how you're gonna patch things up with the family, eh?"

Grover grinned weakly. "Well, I might have an answer for that yet, Boyo. Not all the stuff I'm bringin' is fer me. Got the old lady some little trinkets, too. Thought that might help smooth things over."

"Sounds smart," he agreed, followed by a moment of doubt. "What did you get her?"

Grover stroked his scraggly face. "Let's see... there was a twenty-foot windsock, an ice auger and a bass drum." He shrugged. "Basic woman stuff."

Art quickly made up his mind not to ask what he may have picked out for his kids. "Well, good luck to you. I think you'll need it."

"No more than you, Boyo. In fact, of the two of us, I'd say I fared best. It is a piteous shame, about your Mantid client."

"My *client's* client, you mean," Art corrected. "I performed *my* miracle. Whether Horus pulls his off or not – money's already in the bank."

Grover gave him a look.

"Alright," Art waved his hands defensively. "You got me... I feel bad for the bug, too."

Grover grinned. "You're decent folk, Art Mallard. Thanks fer all ya done."

"Couldn't have done it without you, friend," Art replied, giving a little salute. "See ya in the funny papers."

Grover waved back. Then, turning and looking suddenly apprehensive, started a cautious journey up the ramp...

Art stood there with his hands in his pockets until he saw Grover had made it safely into the bomber. All the while, he grew morose – feeling like a loose strand between two stories forking apart... each to their own, sad ending. Grover would likely go on now to distinguish himself in the world of science... and be a worse outcast among his loved ones and countrymen for it. And now, he'd been reminded of *the bug*. Granted, he'd never even met Horus' latest client, but that didn't make him incapable of sympathy. What really bothered him, though, was the thought of how Horus would handle the defeat. They'd been friends for years now; Art knew a case like this would weigh on him. And all this after Art had 'performed his miracle'. There was nothing quite as depressing as a miracle that went nowhere. He kicked a stone over as he turned to go...

...He had to stop himself abruptly, finding one of the diminutive Phage – the Postmaster General himself – was standing there in his path.

"Capital to see you again, Mr. Mallard," General Rutherford said. "Very good of you to send Mr. Grover off." He turned himself to and fro, searching about. "And what of your other friend, the linguist? Does he not wish to return to Maenea presently?"

"It's partially on his account I'm here," Art explained. "He can't come, General. Not tonight. Seems he'll be tied up with the justice department for a while yet... getting executed."

"Oh my," the General mused. "Well, perhaps we can come back for him later. But for now, we really must see Grover home on schedule."

Art huffed. "It still amazes me you stayed on long enough to give him the round trip." He squinted searchingly. "Just what sorta debt has he been holding over you guys all this time, anyway?"

The little tails around the General's collar turned upward in a sort of alien shrug. "Very little... besides the greatest debt of all." His answer caused Art no small perplexity...

"What's that?"

"The debt of continual goodwill to every soul."

Art itched the back of his head uncomfortably, having forgot that by talking to a postman – *the* Postman, no less – he was carrying on a conversation with some kind of a zealot. "That *is* a big debt. I can't imagine how you came to owe it."

"By choice, mostly." The General stepped up onto his ramp then, and as he did so, a powerful current of oration ionized the atmosphere about him. "If something is on a man's heart, so that he feels he must put pen to paper or send along some token, we facilitate the message, never mind the distance or danger. Nor do we make exception, looking at man or message. Even to O'nyxon himself, we dare extend our services – both incoming and outgoing – and this knowing how he once abused the privilege, to great calamity. We do this because we respect that we do not fathom all the secret things... nor have we catalogued every impulse that would incite a man to scrawl his thoughts into words – words he deems ought to be read by some recipient. But we know this much: among these impulses are care, compassion, and camaraderie, which the intervening of time and many miles has not diminished. And rather than hinder one word of kindness, we would give every letter the benefit of the doubt. For if the very blackest heart were to arrive at only one such word in his life, we should not deny him the chance to convey it – and to do so in confidence." He sighed. "I cannot adequately describe the solemn charge we uphold... this is but the best that I can manage on a whim."

Art shook his head with incredulity. "I... I don't understand all that jazz."

"Never fear, my good man," the General replied. "Perhaps someday you will." His fluffy cape flourished regally as he spun and started on his way.

About the time he was halfway up, Art had a sudden thought. "Oh, General!" he called out, reaching into his coat for his notepad and pen. "Wait just a minute."

Rutherford turned back, his capsule tilting quizzically. "Something the matter, Mr. Mallard?"

"No, but... have you got an envelope on you, by any chance?"

"But of course!" he said, quick-drawing an envelope from his cape fast enough to shame a Festian Desert gunfighter. By then, Art was already busy scrawling...

"Thanks," he said, taking the envelope after a moment more of writing on his pad. A few moments more and he had the address down. He ripped out his note, folded it into the envelope, and lick-sealed it. Then he held it out to Rutherford. "Here ya go. One more for the solemn charge, if you don't mind too much."

"I should say not!" he laughed. "Only too glad to oblige you in the way we know best." He jumped in astonishment, however, as he saw the address on the envelope. "But... this is Mr. Grover's address! Are you quite sure you don't want to simply hand it to him now, yourself, while he yet tarries in Jast-Madiir?"

"It's not for Grover," Art explained. "It's for the Mrs. Call it an act of goodwill." He was the next to jump as he remembered something unaddressed, reaching into jingling pockets. "One more sec... I'll front you the dough for a stamp..."

Rutherford held out a limb. "No need to trouble about it, sir. This one's on the house." When his tiny bug-like legs had carried him all the way to the bomber's hatch, he turned back a final time. "I would not long linger here, Mallard, if I were you. As at our first meeting, we are in for some rain."

Chapter 15

It wasn't until the first droplets drew him back to reality that he realized he'd already heard the thunder. It seemed there was a decision to make here: Either he could shuffle out from beneath the streetlamp and go stand under the long eaves of the train station... or he could stand in place and get soaked. But as one impassive moment stretched into another and the entire question began to fade from memory, the choice seemed clear enough...

In the end, though, the whole thing was taken out of his hands once again. Before he could get too wet, he heard a click and a *whoosh* just behind him. As he started and turned around, he found Deborah at his side, holding an umbrella over his head. She grinned, extending the handle toward him. Hesitantly, he reached for it...

"Thank you anyway..." Horus said, his hand stopping short as he tried to wave her down, "...but really, keep it. You should be the one..."

He was interrupted as she deployed a second umbrella for herself. He took the first with a wry smile. "Inclement weather indeed. If only I'd known before that you could perform miracles."

"No miracles," Deborah replied. "Just good forecasting."

Horus' eyes narrowed. "There were no weathermen calling for rain tonight."

"Oh really?" she asked coyly. "Must be none of them have any rheumatism just behind their left knee."

He nodded. "Must be." Deborah certainly had a way of cheering him in the unfortunately frequent dregs of his profession. But the night was dark beneath cloud and shadow, and the rain was really hemming them in now. Almost immediately he succumbed again to drear and deep reflection. Deborah tried to nudge him back out of it...

"Don't let it eat at you, Horus. You knew from the start the State wouldn't give you this one."

Eyes still fixed on some uncertain point in the distance, Horus shook his head. "We just learned so much. Now we're burdened with it. I know Aphelo isn't dangerous. I believe he's never used those claws to attack anything in his life. But I can't get anyone else to see that." He looked down at her, seeing his words take the starch out of her, making him feel worse. Rather than make her try to dream up some further condolences, he quickly devised a way to pivot the conversation. "Oddly enough, though, that's not what's really bothering me. Not right now." He stroked his chin. "It's such a small thing. Perhaps the smallest thing..."

"What is it?"

"I can't get past what it could have been that made Hamilton act like he was treading on eggshells every time the Monroes came up. It was apparent to me that he was avoiding Michelle's testimony... even though it strengthened his case. Why would he do that?"

"Have you thought about asking him?"

Horus regarded her. "Not seriously." He kept studying her, trying to discern some sarcasm. "Do you really suppose I should, at this hour?"

"You know, Boss," she began, "I take a lot of notes in my line of work... and some of them are even on paper. One thing I've noted: When something's sticking in your craw, it always winds up being worth looking into."

This time, as he smiled at his secretary, there was no half-hearted reservation about it. He didn't know how or why, but there was an obvious course of action ahead of him now. He *would* go search out Blackforest... find his answers... and somehow – unaccountably – emerge enlightened...

"What did I ever do without you?" he dared to ask.

Deborah gave him another signature grin. "You lost most of your cases. But then, some things never really change, do they?"

* * *

Horus' small shoes echoed into the reception lobby of the SAPD, the din of heavy rain and thunder dully droning on outside. No one and nothing really seemed to take note of his appearing... he was greeted only by a vast emptiness. Things always did tend to slow down at police headquarters after dark. It was well understood – even by the city's basest ne'er-do-wells – that committing crimes at night was cliché, and a sophisticated metropolis like St. Argonsburg should be somehow beyond that. Thus, Horus was unsurprised to find only a familiar note hanging over the front of the check-in desk: "Regular business hours resume in the morning. In case of emergency, please ring bell (Horus had never seen a bell). Unless otherwise assisted, please wait here to be processed. No loitering."

Leaving his umbrella to dry, reflexively shaking away the damp cold, Horus continued undeterred on his way to the DA's office...

Here, too, silence prevailed. Only a few lamps were left burning, and as Horus investigated, not one of them was in Blackforest's personal office. He tried the doorhandle, intent to confront his counterpart even in the rare case he was actually sleeping. *Locked.* The DA was out. Horus shook the handle again in a sort of disbelief. Instinct had led him here – or more precisely, Deborah's instinct about his instinct. And if there was one thing that shouldn't fail either an attorney or a secretary – let alone both – it was instinct. *How could Hamilton not be here*?

"Bad form, Templar," he heard a feminine voice confront him. He whirled, but the source was nowhere to be seen. "If a juror can be shot for discussing a case out of court, I'm not sure what business you think you have gabbing with Blackforest now."

Horus backtracked nonchalantly. He hadn't even consciously registered whose office still had the light on... but naturally, it would be hers...

"Ms. Cordon," Horus acknowledged her, leaning into her doorway. She didn't look up from her desk this time... assuming she ever had. "I admit I had hoped I'd find your boss here. Perhaps It's just a carry-over from when we used to discuss mock-trials in law school. Old habits die hard."

"They can *kill* equally hard, if you're not careful," she cautioned, eyes dancing across an array of documents all the while. "But then, I suppose there's no actual language in gag-order statutes that pertain to council. You can sit in here and wait for him, if you're really feeling that nostalgic." She gestured absently at a seat in her office. "He shouldn't be long."

"You know where he is?" Horus asked, even as he sat down.

"Most of the time. Right now he's downstairs debriefing Captain Alexei on an operation the police just conducted in one of our 9th District mines."

"A mine job? That's rather strange. What business did the SAPD have in a mine?"

"They were there to enforce a state order to redistribute the structural bracing."

"Not enough guarding down there?"

"Too much. The mine hasn't been profitable enough to keep investing in bracing for new veins. So engineers were sent in to see about spreading the existing bracing a bit thinner. Our boys were just there to ensure cooperation from the steel miners." She flipped some pages on her desk.

"*Steel* miners?" Horus repeated doubtfully. "Surely the Czarina must realize steel is *forged*... it's not just dug out of the ground..."

Cordon shrugged, still reading a mile a minute. "Small wonder, then, that the mine's been unprofitable."

"I suppose so," Horus said, his attention beginning to wander to whatever it was that had her so preoccupied. "And what is it you're up to tonight, if I may ask?"

"I'm reading all the transcripts from cases in Cape Deltrix that established legal precedent, starting at the oldest and the most recent, and working my way inward from both ends... then back out again."

Horus blinked. "It gives me a headache just to think about that. What on earth would inspire you to do such a thing?"

"The Boss says he wants me to know all these cases forwards and backwards. So that's exactly what I'm working on."

"How very literal," Horus said, arriving at no more polite conclusion.

"What about you, Templar?" she inquired airily, putting the ball back in his court. "What's troubling you now that can't wait till tomorrow?"

"Just something peculiar your boss did... or rather, avoided doing. He carted the Monroes all the way up here, then tried to make his case without them." He laughed once to himself. "Deborah actually encouraged me to come ask; now that I'm here, I do feel rather silly about it. Even so, the question remains with me: Why did Hamilton dance all around the testimony of a key witness?"

"For the same reason you declined to impeach her testimony... obviously," Cordon answered. Horus was taken aback. "He'd elected not to expose their capital crime, if he could avoid it."

Horus shifted his weight forward in his chair. "I had no idea Michelle Monroe's injury was such an open secret. It's surprising enough to learn Hamilton knew... apparently he saw fit to share that information with you as well."

"You've got that the wrong way 'round, Templar. I took the Monroes' statement for Blackforest when they arrived here... and after all, your detective Mallard isn't the only one with a nose."

Horus smiled, even if a bit nervously. "Well, it seems this trip wasn't a waste after all. I'll be sure to thank our friend the DA for exercising such humanitarian discretion." Here came the nervous part. "But what about you? What do *you* intend to do with your knowledge of their crimes?"

"Not a thing." She loudly flipped more sheets of paper. "I think I have quite enough on my plate already."

Horus' smile redoubled: Something in her aggressive dismissiveness gave her away... "Why, Ms. Cordon... I do believe you *care*."

At that, she froze and looked up, appearing rather shocked. Horus detected the faintest whiff of something like a shy grin before she returned, fully-stoic, to her studies. "Think what you like, Counselor. Maybe, if I'd had your job, I might've learned to care about the little people. But I hope not. At any rate, the Boss didn't see fit to throw the Monroes to the raptors. That was *his* decision to make... and I'll stand by it. More than that... the police report has one 'Mich' Monroe hunting, and one foraging... which both satisfies the law as well as reflects the truth. That's more than enough for me."

Horus got up. "There's a budding emancipator in you yet, Blucille. Cape Deltrix will be fortunate to have you." Having his answers, and a passably more hopeful outlook in general, he was prepared to go. Surely, there was nothing left to be gained...

"...What really gets me is that *you* didn't call her out." The ADA stopped him in the doorway with her words. "You passed up your best chance to shift the blame in the case. Why was that, Templar? Could it be that you have a bit of prosecutor in *you*? Be honest... is there some tiny piece of the dogged Defender that wants to see the bug face the firing squad?"

Horus' jowls clung to his teeth. That was a low blow. "Not in the least." He sighed, letting the revulsion at the thought pass. "But I suppose you'd never know it, as thoroughly as I've bungled this case. Hamilton picked my linguist apart. Now, I'm frankly at a complete loss. It might have helped, if I could have at least given my opening statement..."

Cordon half-snickered. "I can only imagine what good that would've done. What were you going to do? Spring-board into an impassioned plea that the Czarina swallow her pride and see reason?"

...Swallow her pride...

...The phrase struck Horus dumb...

This was *it*...

This was that moment of enlightenment he'd hoped for... that impossible but essential moment when the universe plucked his noggin like a tuning fork...

"Her *pride*?" he chanted back to her, fingers tumbling with transient nodes of thought. "Yes... yes, of course. That's been the key to this whole thing all along. You as much as said so from the start..."

She looked up again and grimaced. She watched him for a long interval, inviting some explanation. "Well, don't just stand there, acting so disgustingly inspired. What are you babbling about?"

"A change of heart, Ms. Cordon. A chance to embrace that alleged inner prosecutor. The Czarina believes she wants an execution… I think I can give her one better."

"Like what?"

He grinned his most devious.

"A battle to the death."

Chapter 16

Horus greeted the following night with an air of confidence that hadn't diminished noticeably since his epiphany. Court had yet to be convened, and already he'd received dubious looks from Blackforest and Neferib alike. Even Deborah, who had launched his little quest for inspiration, seemed to regard him as if he might be ill...

Perhaps he was at that. The gambit he had in mind was far from sure to succeed. In the first place, it depended on the Vizier not to knock him down at the very proposition – a longshot in and of itself. Secondly – and quite critically – he had to consider The Pillbox. Was the Czarina here tonight? Would she even bother entertaining a meaningless advocation for the object of her wrath? As ever, Horus had no way to be sure. Or rather, he had only *one way* to be sure. Everything – that which he could influence, as well as the countless things he could not – would have to go over perfectly...

"Court will come to order," Vizier Neferib commanded. Just like the night before, Horus watched as Aphelo was conjured by gong-strike to be put on slowly-spinning exhibition. He did so with hope and intention of seeing him out of those silly restraints within the next few minutes, whether for better or worse...

"Let the defense call his first witness," Neferib declared. "Or, more precisely, his second."

"Thank you, your Honor," Horus grinned as he rose, a roguish glint in his eye as he scanned for his unsuspecting quarry. It had taken some effort to arrange for him to be present tonight, but as Horus finally homed-in on the battered shape of the man, he was reaffirmed to see his plan continuing to foment...

"I call Captain Alexei to the stand."

The police captain, after a healthy interval of looking equal parts horrified and flabbergasted, stood and limped on his stilted legs down to the performance level. Horus could see that the previous night's operation had taken its own physical toll on Alexei. Not undeservedly, he felt shame at the thought of all he was about to subject the man to. But after all, he knew of no one more predisposed to go along with such a stunt...

When all proper protocol had been observed, and Alexei seated, Horus meandered up to the witness stand. "Now, Captain," he started, fiddling with a pen from his table. "Before we launch headlong into the unpleasant business ahead, I think we should take a moment to acquaint the court with you. What is your line of work?"

He cleared his throat, first quietly, then much louder – calibrating his voice for a most unexpected public address. "I'm a police captain, in the St. Argonsburg Police Department."

"How long have you been with the SAPD?"

He ran the numbers in the air in front of himself. "A month, five weeks, and three days. No – two."

"And in that time, how many injuries have you incurred?"

He laughed nervously – the sound caught in his throat. "I haven't kept close record, sir."

"But they've been frequent?"

Alexei shrugged. "Perhaps. I am still getting accustomed to the demands of big-city work, being from rather a small burg, myself. I would not know precisely if my misfortunes were relatively frequent or infrequent."

"Very well – let us instead pursue this matter by case-study. Were you injured on your most recent assignment?"

He nodded. "Yes, sir."

"Could you describe what happened?"

His eyes rolled skyward as he thought back. "Well, we were on security detail in this mine, you see. And all of a sudden – unaccountably – a mining cart came barreling down a slope in the track, full bore! Seeing that it might do harm to a group of my fellow officers if left to its course, I did my best to obstruct the thing with the only impediment I could contrive to fling in the way on short notice."

"Yourself, you mean."

"Yes."

Horus put the pen away, leaning an arm on the stand. "It would seem to me, Captain, as if you have a remarkable willingness to risk life and limb in the service of law and order."

Alexei smiled, a bit embarrassed. "That would have to be *your* assessment, sir... I only do what seems dutiful."

"Your Honor," Blackforest interjected. "Grounding the court in a few pertinent details about a witness is one thing... the defense seems to be trying to construct an entire *psychological profile*. Where is the relevancy? What meaningful connection does this have witness with the defendant?"

"I've been wondering that myself," Alexei squeaked, almost inaudibly.

"I beg the court's indulgence," Horus appealed. "I have merely been trying to establish the suitability of this man to assist me in a demonstration."

"What kind of demonstration?" Neferib asked, brow furrowed. Horus couldn't help feeling the weight of that question bearing down on him from all gathered...

"...It is my intention to pit my client against this witness in mortal combat."

"Objection!" Blackforest winged reflexively. Everyone turned to regard him, his wide eyes searching for something more to say. "I... that is..." He seethed, at a complete loss. "Well, never *mind*! Suppose the defense helps us understand what he could possibly be thinking, so I can object properly."

Neferib shifted back to Horus, her look questioning, but otherwise impassive. "For what purpose would you be conducting this demonstration, Counselor?"

Horus leveled a stern look at Blackforest. "I concede the State has presented a good case, up to a point... he has shown opportunity, agency, and hostile intent. But have we done anything thus far to demonstrate *how* the crime was committed? Have we proposed to explain *how* this Mantid – or those like him – has defamed the crown with their prowess in battle? That is what the defense means to examine with this demonstration. I mean to recreate, for the benefit of the court, a deadly encounter between Human and Mantid. I strongly believe that to do so will be inherently enlightening."

"Your Honor," Blackforest began again, more delicately, as he approached the bench. "If I didn't know better, I'd say the defense is actually *trying* to pad my case. In that light, I'm loath to follow through with an objection. But as far as a re-creation of battlefield conditions, this arrangement leaves much to be desired." He nodded in Alexei's direction. "This man is a policeman, not a soldier."

Horus was not about to be stymied. "Captain, do you have skill with a musket?"

"We do receive very basic drilling with the weapon, as part of police training." His expression was not exceedingly confident. Horus was encouraged.

"And are you willing to accept the risk of a battle to the death, for the benefit of the court?"

Now, he looked very unsure indeed. "Well, I... I suppose..."

"Thank you, Captain," Horus nodded appreciatively. "You see, your Honor, my choice is not entirely unfounded."

The Vizier folded her arms. "You puzzle me, Counselor. What have you to gain from your proposition here? If your client wins, he makes himself liable to a very demonstrable charge of murder, on top of his existing allegations. But if he loses, then the State's sentence will have been carried out by default. In what way are you representing your client's best interests? That *is* your charge, in case you've forgotten..."

"Not at all," Horus asserted. "I must admit that at this point, clearing my client of the charges against him is probably impossible. He is definitely, unquestionably, a natural-born killer, far exceeding any possible Human rival. But there is more than one way of representing his best interests. If my ability to defend him legally has run its course, I can at least try to give him a final chance to defend his own honor, as part of a warlike society. If, in the process, I happen to explore an unprecedented opportunity to learn something of our enemies – how they have managed to so humiliate us throughout the centuries – and reinforce the State's body of evidence as well, that can hardly be helped. The way I see it, I'm acting in *everyone's* best interests... with the minor exception of this police captain."

Vizier Neferib sat back, scratching under her chin while she mulled it all over. Horus waited breathlessly. Everything had already been put on the table. If she didn't go along with it, Horus would have to rest his case, having no less personally asserted that his client was a living weapon. And even if she *did* go along with it, things could still go **horribly** wrong...

"Very well," she answered finally, turning to the bailiffs. "The defendant will be loosed from his restraints and instructed to attack this witness. But do not unbind his wings." She shot Horus an icy glance. "Let us not be so quick to oblige the defense that we inadvertently let his client go free."

Horus grinned nervously. It certainly would have been a handy misfortune if, in the process of arranging the battle, Aphelo was let a little too loose and managed to simply fly away. He honestly wished he'd thought of that...

"I will need my translator brought forward to explain this to my client, your Honor," Horus explained.

"Indeed," the Vizier said, looking into the audience, finding the ghostly form of Jojojo present. "I am pleased to see he managed to be punctual this time."

"Yes, your Honor... I have learned my lesson," Jojojo replied.

"Good. Please come forward. Confer with the defendant."

While Jojojo related the situation to Aphelo, Horus stole a moment to speak with Alexei. "Sorry to put you up to this on short notice, Captain. The idea only struck me the night before. Even so, I hope you'll oblige me with a small favor. Please do your best not to hurt my client. Focus on defending yourself."

Alexei watched with thinly veiled horror as a bailiff handed him a musket. "I'm not greatly encouraged to know that you're working both corners, Mr. Templar," he said absently.

"You just have to trust me, Alexei. And, besides that... you have to fight your worst."

He blanched. "Don't you mean, my *best*?"

Horus grinned. "In a way, yes. Give it your best, *worst* fight."

"O dearly departed Creators," Alexei breathed. "What have I stepped into?"

Just as Horus turned away, the apparition of Jojojo floated up to him. "Aphelo is fully advised of the situation."

Horus nodded. "Was it very difficult to explain?"

Jojojo motioned with his tentacles in a sort of shrug. "I could not render his accent well without benefit of my accessories. Otherwise, it was a simple matter. He actually told me this was the most sensible turn he's had since he was captured."

Horus was very pleased. "Wonderful. Thank you... 'Yo-ho-jo'?"

"Why, Mr. Templar," Jojojo marveled, "I do believe you've stated my name correctly."

* * *

After a flurry of activity so fluid, one might have believed that these sorts of demonstrations were put on in court all the time, Alexei and Aphelo were standing silently opposite one another, amid the pillars on the performance level of the amphitheatre. It was a tense atmosphere, with all present swept suddenly into the breathless anticipation of a truly unforgettable spectacle. They would be the first to witness the timeless battle of man versus Mantid, and live to tell of it...

Horus, being the de facto ringleader of this: the greatest show on earth, stepped out into their midst... the very center of the arena. "Let the demonstration commence," he declared. Ad-libbing, the executioner with the gong affirmed the command...

Alexei thrust the musket out in front of himself, his gangly features adopting a comically wide stance as he set into a slow, declining orbit. His face was aflutter, trying to look fierce without benefit of a single muscle that knew how to do so. Or, perhaps he was simply squinting to account for his present lack of glasses...

Aphelo, for his part, was every bit as underwhelming out of the gate. He didn't seem to have any prior experience side-stepping – the very act of the two of them circling each other appeared to tax his motor skills. He had his claws, which might have been an intimidating feature, except for how he used them. Rather than simply extend, he kept opening and closing them in a kind of 'clip-clop, clip-clop' pattern. It seemed more like he was trying to lay down a beat than offer some meaningful warning. More likely than not, that was *exactly* what he was doing, so that he could avoid tripping over himself...

The two combatants circled... and circled. After that, they circled some more. Once, it looked like they might commit to some action, but they both seemed to interpret whatever had happened as a misstep, and simply began circling again in the other direction...

And all the while, the atmosphere of tension melted into boredom...

The Captain and the Mantid did, however, slowly inch forward in their endless traverse. About the time they were ten yards apart, Alexei had his musket so far out ahead of himself that none could really understand how he managed to avoid falling face forward in the dirt. Aphelo had mastered sidestepping well enough by this point – having already amassed virtual eons of practice since the battle's onset – that his forelegs were now held out in what may have come across as a frightening defensive posture... if they weren't shaking so bad. Meanwhile, both men had unconsciously turned their heads several degrees away from each other, as if to be ready to avert their gaze when the inevitable deathblow was struck at them...

Horus allowed this to continue until he himself could hardly endure the monotony. "The subjects will now attack!" he announced.

The fighters obliged reflexively with a flying leap. They fell well short of each other and scantily avoided a synchronized faceplant. But they were committed now... and actually closed to what they must have honestly seemed like striking distance. They traded faux lunges, trying to bait the other. They often nearly took the bait, only to awkwardly wrangle themselves back in a flailing ball, fearing a counterstrike that always came much too late, if it came at all...

"Here we see the stalking technique of the Dire Mantid at work," Horus began to narrate on a whim. "It is a fearful and disorienting dance. By this time, even our most battle-tested soldiers must surely lose their nerve..."

Alexei gave a battle-cry and committed to an actual strike, apparently in a fierce denial of his own dread, which Horus had described aptly enough. The hit landed... if not soundly. He had glancingly rapped Aphelo on the foreleg with the barrel of his musket. The bug chittered what must surely have been a blue streak as he hopped back in circles, cradling the bruise in a way that was universally reminiscent of a man who'd gone to strike a nail with a hammer and found his thumb instead...

"The creature's impervious exoskeleton allows him to completely disregard even the most grievous blows," Horus captioned.

When he got over the initial throbbing agony, Aphelo mustered himself, surely committing to a final effort to go down swinging. He leapt, and lashed... with all the embarrassing lethargy of a half-frozen lizard. Horus changed his mind and decided he was glad Aphelo's wings had been left bound... anything the insect might have known about leaping clearly did not apply when he could only do it with his legs. Alexei evaded one attack after another with no apparent effort... only a look of shock mingled with confusion, as if trying to discern whether he was still in an *actual* mortal contest. Most of the audience shared the look. The mood had progressed beyond boredom to something like the hypnosis of being unable to avert one's eyes from the scene of an accident. Only instead of being so entranced by dread-fascination, it was more like the battle was so painfully humiliating that it was impossible not to watch...

"See what speed and precision his feral attacks boast. What raw and utterly fearsome might he commands."

Aphelo pressed his attacks. Alexei, growing tired – and perhaps bored – of simply avoiding the strikes, began to block them, having time and to spare with which to anticipate each one. Aside from a lone cut on a finger, he carried on for what seemed minutes on end without injury. As the battle wore on, Aphelo's movements went from sluggish to glacial. He had probably never exerted himself so much in his whole life, committing total-body strength to every failed strike. Both men, completely without real prior combat experience, were beginning to droop with exhaustion, their every breath a dramatic heave. Had they not both been in possession of something razor-sharp, they would not have any longer had the means of inflicting any harm on each other at all...

Finally, when it seemed impossible that anyone could further bear the sight of the two pooped-out opponents failing more and more absolutely to demonstrate any carnage worth watching, the Vizier stood, a royal message-runner being found by her bench...

"Stop this!" she ordered. "You must desist your demonstration at once... by decree of the Czarina."

The fighters froze. Aphelo collapsed. Horus turned slowly toward the judge. *He'd done it.* All that was left was to cross the finish line with a bit of professionalism...

"Pardon me, your Honor?"

She remained standing, gavel in hand. "You heard me, Counselor. This exhibition is finished... as is the trial. Her Highness has determined that the defendant is much too pitiful a creature to be considered a bitter adversary... that his execution as such would be an insult to the dignity of the country, and the throne. She orders that all charges in the case of Jast-Madiir vs. the Mantid be dropped. Thus speaks your Czarina."

Neferib clacked her gavel against the table.

Nothing happened in the immediate aftermath. Disbelief, as well as a myriad of other, nameless disappointments, held the general populace in a brief suspended animation. But as reality slowly set in, and the room softly bubbled into the speechless sound of hundreds of dejected onlookers martialing themselves out of the Judicature, Horus allowed himself a cleansing sigh. He actually *had* done it. He'd won the fight of his life... by arranging for his client to botch his own...

By the time he finished basking in it, most everyone was gone. But, as he looked over... Horus saw that did not include Blackforest. The DA was still sitting back, studying Aphelo, who remained panting on the ground. While Horus watched, Blackforest stood and slowly crossed the distance between them, until he was kneeling right over the bug. Almost without a thought, Horus joined him there...

"Did you poison him?" Blackforest asked, at great length.

"No," Horus laughed, the question finally clicking. "The little guy's just tuckered out. He'll be fine."

Blackforest trained his searching look on Horus – it was one of the stronger ones in his arsenal, so that Horus could not have lied to him...

"What was the trick, then?"

"No tricks, Hamilton," Horus assured him. "Or, if there was *any* trick, it was getting him this chance to show us the true measure of his menace."

Blackforest's jaw shifted. He examined Aphelo once more. Then, a knowing look tugging at his features, his gaze shifted back. He nodded. "Well done, Horus. Very well done."

With that affirmation, he stood and walked away.

As the prosecution retired, Horus turned back to his client, resting a hand gently on his shoulder-joint. "It'll be alright now, Aphelo," he said. "You won't understand, but I wanted to be the first to tell you. It's going to be alright."

If it were possible, the Mantid's slack form on the ground seemed to go slacker. He was more than just exhausted now. He was *relaxed*. Horus was glad. Aphelo knew what Horus had told him. Somehow, he knew...

Chapter 17

A blast on the train whistle issued the melancholy warning to the world: Five minutes to departure. The long shadows of evening gathered all the richest colors up into the sky, beyond his view. The dedicated car three spaces ahead began to mumble its nightly trumpet sonata. Horus stood and walked over to his blinds, purposing to close them down, just as if he was about to pass any old somnolent night...

...But as he reached the window, he looked out. As before, there was a damsel already looking back. This time, however, the deep dark eyes that met his were Deborah's. Horus nodded before releasing the blinds. Then he crossed the room again, stepped through his monogramed door and met her at the boarding stairs...

"I didn't expect you to be so encumbered," he said.

She held out a big heavy package wrapped in parchment. "We're in the meat, Boss," she replied. "Another special order."

"Very generous, even for a long trip."

She shrugged. "Whatever he doesn't want can always sit in the desk drawer a few weeks."

Horus laughed. "Well, never mind generosity. Very mercenary of you." He tilted his head. "Would you like a hand with that?"

"I wouldn't mind," she answered, handing the meat off. Even as he took it, his eyes were drawn to another mystery...

"What's that under your other arm?"

"The paper."

He gave her a quizzical look. "Surely not the one from tomorrow... at *this* early hour?"

"Hardly. It's the one from four days ago." She unrolled it, joining him on the car's veranda. It shimmered and warbled, rather than crinkling. "I got it laminated. It's going up in the office."

Horus shook his head. "Might it be a dubious precedent to start displaying my own achievements?"

"It's not for *your* office. You can exercise whatever modesty you want, Boss. I for one would like a reminder that I work for a winner." She held it out for him to see. "I don't suppose you've even read the story yet."

He obliged her and read it. "'Defense Wins Notable Victory in Mantid Trial'." He had a doubletake. "*Notable*? But isn't that an adjective?"

Deborah looked away a bit uncomfortably as she rolled the paper back up. "Yeah. Incidentally, you might be getting a job representing a newsman in a day or two."

Horus blanched. He rubbed the back of his neck. "Lovely."

"Anyway, let's get this stuff in the car; Art's going to be along momentarily."

"I didn't know he was coming." Horus took out a timepiece as he pushed back into his office. "The guest of honor had better be along momentarily, too. The train won't wait."

"Not to worry," Deborah said, coming in behind him. "The Deputy Constable assured me he'd be sending him in care of his best and brightest."

"Did someone say, 'best and brightest'?" Art asked, sticking his head in the door, taking them both by surprise.

"Well hello, Art," Deborah intoned. "I told Horus you'd be along in just a moment... I didn't know how right I was!"

"Good to have you, Art," Horus added. "We've hardly touched base since you got back from Maenea."

"How did your date with Blucille go?" Deborah asked suddenly.

Art finished letting himself into the office car, giving Deborah a defensive look. "It wasn't a *date*. It was an *appointment*."

Horus grinned. "I didn't know about this. What did you have an appointment with her for?"

"To set up a date," Art explained.

"Well... *how did it go*?" Deborah insisted.

Art made a quick, crestfallen examination of the floor. "She turned me down flat. But I'm not discouraged! Something about the way she did it without even looking up from her typewriter made it obvious: She really digs me."

Deborah appeared unconvinced. "Sure she does."

"Hey, give a private eye some credit. I'm a good judge of character. And my verdict on Blucille is: She's a good judge of character, too." His eyes bugged, and he went for a pocket in his coat. "Which reminds me – I got a letter from Grover today." He fished it out, still in a pristine envelope...

"You haven't opened it yet?" Horus asked.

"I was saving it for the occasion," he explained, lancing through the top with a sharp claw. Horus and Deborah looked on as he unfolded and quickly read the letter to himself, a smile cracking as he went.

"Well?" Deborah pried at length.

"All's well on the Maenean front," Art reported. "Jojojo's notes were enough to square things with the journal. Grover's a respected scientist now. Better yet... his wife took him back."

Horus stroked his whiskers, bemused. "Two happy endings that would have seemed irreconcilable. How do you suppose he managed it?"

Art turned his chin up smugly. "I wouldn't know anything about the science stuff... but the rest was all me."

"Oh?" Deborah humored him. "Do tell."

"It was elementary. All Grover really needed was someone to advocate for him. So that's just what I did. I sent his wife my fairly-honest voucher in the mail. I told her he was A-OK."

Horus shook his head. "You really think the unsolicited character reference of a complete stranger was enough to save their marriage?"

He shrugged. "Stranger things have happened, Horus. Anyway, it couldn't have been those terrible gifts he bought her."

In the next moment, they were interrupted by a knock at the door. Deborah reflexively went to open it...

As she did, they found Deputy Constable Stenya Miloje himself darkening Horus' doorway.

"Good evening, Milo," Horus greeted him. "Deborah *did* tell me you had your best and brightest coming."

"So why do you all look so surprised to see me?" Miloje asked, removing his hat as he came into the car.

"Well, this is a rather small formality for a Deputy Constable, don't you think?"

"Not at all. However anticlimactic the finish, this is still the case of the century. Besides, I wouldn't miss a good reprise."

Horus leveled a more serious look at him. "It's just as well you're here – I've been meaning to talk to you about something."

"Oh dear," Miloje reacted, feigning disquiet. "Have I walked unwittingly into a browbeating from the star attorney?"

Horus folded his arms, barricading himself against the sarcasm. "It's about Captain Alexei. The man's a danger to himself, Milo. Surely, you've noticed. *I have*... and to my shame, I've even taken advantage of it. It has to stop – here and now – before he has an accident he doesn't walk away from. But I don't believe it *will* stop... unless you stop it. He's been taking all this damage to prove himself to *you*, you know."

"Oh yes... I know *that*. But that doesn't stop me finding it annoying."

No one offered a word of reply. They just eyed the Deputy Constable. He tumbled his bobby in his hands as the pressure started to get to him...

"...In point of fact, Templar, I have already found occasion to have a chat with the lad." His eyes were fixed down with notable solemnity. "That little trip into the mine might have resulted in my own maiming, had he not stepped in. I've told him since: His place here in the SAPD is secure... and duly earned. I felt I owed him that much."

Horus sighed, another weight lifting from him. "I'm quite relieved to hear it; now I can step away from the case feeling justice has been served to all."

A wily glint came back into Miloje's eye. "You certainly had an interesting way of getting your justice, this time around. That was a bit of unabashed showmanship the average defense attorney only dreams about. Whatever gave you the idea to put on such a stunt?"

Horus laughed it off. "The key was just to finally hear what everyone had been telling me ad nauseum from day one – the case was all about *pride*. After that it was simple – I just had to make it too humiliating for Aphelo to take on the mantle of his people's infamy. But it wasn't enough to tell people what a harmless bug he was... I had to *show* them. If I could do that, I was sure the Czarina would be forced to commute him, just to save face. Fortunately for Aphelo... and Alexei... I was right."

The train whistle interjected its one-minute warning.

"Speaking of your client... perhaps we ought to get him in here, lest we make the impending circuit in vain." Miloje leaned back out the door and signaled to unseen underlings outside. A pair of big policemen appeared shortly thereafter, depositing a familiar duffle...

"You put him back in the bag?" Horus asked.

Miloje shrugged defensively. "It seemed expedient. Commuted or not, he doesn't really need to be shown all around our capitol before we turn him loose. Besides that, it saved the commoners some incredulity, seeing policemen escort a big bug down the streets."

"Very well," Horus replied, "but he'll be discrete enough in here. Let's have him out of the bag..."

With some effort, Horus found Aphelo's way out of the bag himself. The Mantid chittered, fidgeted... but soon enough seemed relaxed, finding an amicable spot to hunker on the ground. Deborah started uncovering the meaty care package she'd brought from the market. Miloje signaled his men the okay to depart.

"There's one more question on my mind," Art announced. "Not that I'm disappointed, but I thought sure Jojojo would be here. Where is the old fussbudget? On his way back to Maenea, I suppose?"

"Oddly, no," Deborah piped up, having knowledge of the situation. "He's planning to go to Roemnar next."

Art's face scrunched up. "*Roemnar*? Why the Heck would he go there?"

"Would you believe: He got a royal summons?" Deborah asked, her voice borderline ominous...

Art looked to Horus for confirmation. He nodded. "Well, they're welcome to him, I say. But that is a real head-scratcher."

"There's no accounting for Herons," Miloje grumbled. "But I'm also surprised the translator is absent. I don't know how you plan to give your client a proper send-off without him."

"Don't worry," Horus assured him, exchanging a look with Deborah. "I've made other arrangements."

* * *

It was hours after dark by the time they had reached the depot at Burtridge – a smaller urban satellite southeast and further up the mountain, which St. Argonsburg had not yet grown large enough to assimilate. From there, the entire party hiked by torchlight another half-hour beyond the edge of town, into wooded wilderness. To their surprise – and momentary horror – Aphelo's eyes mimicked the fire's light. As they trekked ever deeper into the musty forest, welcomed by a sea of cricket-song, it became clear that his spirits had also caught ablaze. Still quite far from home, the Mantid at least felt back in his element. Rather than leading him out of their world, they felt distinctly like he was leading them into his...

Finally, they reached just the sort of milestone they had set out for – an opening in the trees on a ridge in Mt. Norvein, beyond which you could easily spy all that lay to the south. It was an exceptionally clear night, and as they looked out, even the vague shape of Corsicarthal's base could be made out in the southwest, before it marched up into inscrutable haze.

Here, they lingered... all knowing this was where their ways would part. Aphelo stepped out onto the very precipice, wings shifting under their covers with nervous energy. He turned back to face them. The moment was at hand...

"You alluded to some ceremony, Templar," Miloje reminded him.

"Yes," Horus replied, looking on. "It seems the time has come. Let's see if I'm up to it." He handed his torch off to Deborah. "I worked for days to get this just right..."

He joined Aphelo near the edge, getting down on his knees to be at eye-level. He reached into his jacket. As he shifted so one knee was out, a few small instruments came out of his inner pockets... a castanet, and a pair of spoons. What he was about to do was tricky with so few limbs... he would have to hold the castanet hand out so that the arm was over his knee: It was the only way he'd have enough surfaces to slap the spoons against...

After he got in place and took a moment to focus, he set right into it... a rigorously rehearsed series of clicks and clacks – an incredibly short symphony of about a half-second, which nonetheless had to be done precisely right. Even the slightest miscue, and Aphelo might think he had sent him off with the word, "vegetable," or, "jingle". But to Horus' delight, he rattled the pattern off just the way he'd spent many hours trying to perfect. He smiled, feeling a special catharsis in getting to relay his salutation personally.

...But what happened next surprised him. After a moment, Aphelo broke out in some strange noises... almost coughs. As Horus listened, however, the sounds coming from Aphelo's mandibles modulated, until it was uncannily like listening to a man clear his throat. It finally dawned on Horus that his client had prepared a statement of his own...

...He waited...

...And at last, he heard...

"Dear Mr. Horus Templar – it has come to my attention that you've been working with our brilliant and illustrious translator to prepare some parting words. I sincerely appreciate the gesture, and so I've decided to do likewise. But what does one say in a moment such as this? I'm sure I don't know... and anyway, I've never been much for goodbyes, so bear with me. Perhaps a few brief, honest remarks will be enough. Ours has been a bit of a rocky association, as I'm sure you'll agree. There was, of course, the part where you tried to blow me up. Plus, I'll admit to being quite unnerved by the long hours you spent just staring at me. But I know you meant well. And I know I have you to thank for the very fact that I'm alive today... an ironic turn of circumstance from the time I spent convinced you meant to kill me yourself. I *do* thank you, from the very softest hollow of my thorax. You're a man of exceptional character, the likes of which it would be anyone's good fortune to meet. And while my own name might be Aphelo: in my book, you're really

a fellow, too… which our mutual friend assures me is a rip-snorting good pun in your language. Take care, Mr. Templar… and if you ever find yourself in the jungle – which I don't suggest you do – be sure to look me up."

Horus could do naught but stare blankly. At great length, though, he managed a nod.

Aphelo nodded back. And then, with a quick turn and a loud and blustery thrum of wings, he vanished into the night…

They all remained in their places for long seconds afterward, more dumbfounded than solemn.

"Strange," Horus said at length. "I didn't take him for a man of so many words."

"Ya think ya know a guy," Art commiserated. "What was it you said to *him*?"

Horus' face remained utterly blank. "I simply said, 'Goodbye'."

"Well, this whole affair has never strayed far from total disappointment," Miloje sighed. "What now, Horus… besides the long walk back to town?"

Horus got back up. He checked his timepiece. "I see it's half past midnight." He searched their faces, an eager smile returning to his own. "How about an early dinner?"

Acknowledgments

Firstly, I'd like to thank the same exact people as I did in the novel *The Chocolate Prophecy*. If you haven't read those acknowledgments, or the book they're attached to, I cannot be held accountable for that. In particular, though, I'd better reiterate my gratitude to Erle Stanley Gardner. Admittedly, it is the depictions of his characters provided by Raymond Burr, Barbara Hale, William Hopper, William Talman (and now, Ray Collins) that this book owes the most to. I failed utterly to imagine a better legal ensemble cast, and so could only – at best – homage these folks.

Additional special thanks go to my mom, who diligently proofread this book, as well as the aforementioned novel. Thanks, Mom! I would have felt pretty dumb if you hadn't found those errors!

And here's a shout-out to the Tamarack Writers Group! I surely appreciate the interest and support you all gave me as I read along!

Perhaps I should also thank some academy or other, except I don't know which one, or why...

For More from E.L. Ward…

Visit his personal site, at:

https://www.booksofelward.com

His vast arsenal of backlist titles includes the following:

TITLES IN THE ORPHAN UNIVERSE

HERON PROPHECIES SERIES

The Chocolate Prophecy

HORUS TEMPLAR – PUBLIC DEFENDER SERIES

Horus Templar and the Case of the Wimpy War-Criminal
Horus Templar and the Case of the Iniquitous Inquisitor
Horus Templar and the Case of the Draft-Dodging Drone
Horus Templar and the Case of the Dubious Decedent

E.L. Ward is proud to partner with:

MALOB ARTS

Made in the USA
Monee, IL
04 November 2026

67384557R00079